QUIT WHILE
(You Think)
YOU'RE A-HEAD

(More Terrifying Tales of a Teesside Teacher)

PUBLISHING

First Edition published 2019 by
2QT Limited (Publishing)
Settle, North Yorkshire BD24 9RH United Kingdom

Printed in Great Britain by Lightning Source UK Ltd
A CIP catalogue record for this book is available
from the British Library

ISBN 978-1-913071-20-2

QUIT WHILE
(You Think)
YOU'RE A-HEAD

(More Terrifying Tales of a Teesside Teacher)

Bryan Cross

Dedication

Where to start? Well, my first book was dedicated to my family, close friends and many school staff, teaching and non-teaching, plus pupils. The same goes for this, my second book. Again, over the period of writing this book they have been truly supportive and caring, always ready to listen, always ready to give me their praise and critique, be it a 'yeah, go for it' or 'are you sure?'

Certainly a mention for my son Mark who, as in *Quit While You're a-Head* (Book 1) and now in *Quit While (You Think) You're a-Head* (Book 2), gave me much guidance and advice in planning the cover design.

Huge applause too for my dear friend and WI President, Carole Prichard, who has listened daily, so it seems, to my silly ideas and remarks even during my days of feeling down and sad, days when things seemed a bit overwhelming and daunting in all walks of life. I truly could not have coped through the past year without her support – and most certainly I could not have written this, my second book.

Thus, if the book gets a 'bad press', so to speak, or is not well received, I can revert to that well-known phrase… 'Well, she made me do it!'

Of course, besides the personal support from friends and family in writing this book there are so many others who have helped with the production, marketing and sales of my first book. (Yes! A few did get sold.)

Maureen, Frances, Phyllis and Moyra, ex-Grange Primary School, Hartlepool.

Peter Cornforth, Head of Fens Primary School, Hartlepool.

Richard and Mel from Drakes Bookshop in Stockton-on-Tees.

Debbie and Heather from Norton-on-Tees and Fairfield Libraries.

Toni and Staff from Guisborough Bookshop.

Finally, Catherine Cousins and colleagues from 2QT Publishing, Settle, North Yorkshire for their warmth, friendliness and much-needed expertise.

To all these guys, thanks for your support and encouragement. I'm hopeful they will offer their much-needed assistance yet again!

Pipe, armchair and slippers will never be the same.

An Opening Blessing

A simple greeting I read on a plaque placed near a tree planted in memory of a loved one. It is situated by a memorial cross on the 'Howe', looking down on St Michael and St George's Church in Castleton.

> May the road rise up to meet you
> May the wind be always on your back
> May the sun shine warm upon your face
> The rain fall, upon your fields and until
> we meet again
> May God hold you in the palm of His hand.

Before we really get started, may I use this Irish blessing to all those in Castleton and surrounding villages who have shown such warmth and care since I returned to this area in 2017, especially to those in the Castleton and Danby Bowls Club. One of the members, John F. Watson, also had his first novel, *A Journey of Hope,* published in 2018. John is, like me, in his seventh decade. He is a proper writer and his book is well worth a read … after you've read mine, obviously!

In addition, thanks to my Christian friends in the parish; there are too many to mention by name but all are truly supportive and kind.

Finally, to the renowned ukulele group the 'Eskuleles'. Thanks for the laughter and fun during recent months.

The Eskuleles are a group of ukulele players who meet every Wednesday in The Fox and Hounds pub in Ainthorpe on the North York Moors. Most of the members live in the local area of Castleton and Danby, close to the River Esk – hence the name Eskuleles.

The group started back in 2012, when Chris Milns went to his son's ukulele club down south, enjoyed the fun and bought an instrument. Finding there was no club to join locally, he persuaded his good friend, musician Miles Keith, to help him start one. The Fox and Hounds had a games room, plenty of beer on hand and was an obvious venue.

It all began one snowy night in February 2013. About a dozen hardy souls turned up, followed by a few more the next week and so on…

Chris and Miles were ably supported in the running of the club by other founder members and friends, Philip and Lesley, and later by Noel and Sue. Dave Chapman helped teach some of the beginners the basic chords. The club has grown from strength to strength and now has around forty members.

The first gig was held at The Grapes pub, Scaling Dam, in November 2013 and raised £800 for Marie Curie. Many more performances have followed in village halls and at local shows, birthdays and weddings, with around £15,000 in total being raised for charitable causes. The club now raises funds for the Great North Air Ambulance, a vital service for those living on the Moors.

The Eskuleles are far more than just a music club; they contribute to the wellbeing of the village community. Here are a few comments from members: 'so much fun'; 'supportive and friendly atmosphere'; 'made many new friends'; 'highlight of my week'; 'love the banter'; 'so many characters'; 'never thought I'd play a musical instrument'; 'discovered hidden talent'; 'improved my self-confidence'; 'helped me through difficult times'.

Here is a song that I have written as a thank you and a tongue-in-cheek tribute to you all for great camaraderie and happiness during our sessions.

THE PESKY ESKULELES

(sung in a Chas & Dave style. Actions for the chorus are available for a modest fee!)

Chorus
Walk right in, money in the tin,
Drink your whisky, beer or gin.
Sing a lot of songs, make a lot of din,
At the Pesky Eskuleles!

Leadin' us is Banjo 'Joe'.
Miles is fast, Chris is slow! (jokin')
Noel keeps us goin', way down low,
At the Pesky Eskuleles!

Philip and Lesley also in the crew,
She puts the words up – so thank you.
When she's missing we haven't got a clue
At the Pesky Eskuleles!

Pete takes the mike, sure is fun,
Makes us laugh – everyone.
They say he's a 'Thesbian' – oh go on!
At the Pesky Eskuleles!

David at the back, braces on,
Claps and cheers at everyone.
Except maybe – is it Tom?
At the Pesky Eskuleles!

In comes Barbara, lookin' cool.
Always makes the fellas drool.
Was she ever late for school?
At the Pesky Eskuleles!

Danny, Vilna, Paul and John,
Pauline, Tony, everyone…
So many to mention, the list goes on…
At the Pesky Eskuleles!

Contents

Introduction

Since my first book – what? You haven't read it? Get yourself down to your bookseller now before all stocks are gone. In fact, there may be one or two residing in local charity shops, car-boot sales or school-fair jumbles (now, there's irony).

I repeat, since the publication of my first book I have been blessed in meeting a number of ex-pupils, staff and parents. For some strange reason they were keen to see me and, contrary to widespread belief, not to duff me up but to say a cheery hello. Truly it was wonderful to meet them again, some after almost fifty years. Some were married and some have grandchildren so lying about my present age is now, quite clearly, totally impossible!

Meeting up with so many of them triggered off further memories so, by popular demand, another helping of Terrifying Teesside Teacher Tales is ready to be served. Running with the food analogy, these new revelations are not dim recollections – but may be not fit for human consumption or liable to give indigestion. Only time will tell whether they tickle your taste buds.

However, the demand for my first published 'work' has been such that I have bowed to public pressure and been forced to take up my pen once more and produce Book Two for my devoted and loyal – yet demanding – audience. Indeed, such has been the response that, to satisfy my discerning readers, I have ventured out of the school grounds on occasions in my second book. This is to emphasise that the terrifying tales did not confine themselves to within the school but also without, and also when I was a pupil. Yes, school Misses and Sirs were once pupils themselves. Wow, there are some I wouldn't have wanted in my class.

Over the past few months since publication, I have been stopped many times in the street by my readers. However, following a brief struggle and apologetic words, I managed to wriggle free and escape their attentions.

Quit While You're a Writer? Maybe, just maybe.

To close on a serious note (who, me?) I really have been delighted with the response to my initial appearance in print. Seeing your book cover for the first time with your name on it is quite a thrill but, hand on heart, meeting up with some wonderful, special people from years gone by has been remarkable and so much more rewarding. I don't know who got the biggest surprise but I do know who got the biggest enjoyment. What a joy it has been to meet up with so many ex-pupils and to give them a hug. (My goodness, some of them have grown tall!)

When I met Dawn, the 'superstar' girl footballer, and her brother, Ian, the years seemed to roll back and there was so much to chat about. From the same era there is 'Pally' – Gary Pallister. Thanks for your time and the foreword for my first book. (The cheque's in the post.)

Then there was Karen Bates, as she was then called, or 'Katie Batey', as I couldn't resist calling her when she was in my class. She suddenly popped up with her mum and dad. No, I didn't recognise her, but as soon as she said 'Olly Owl' I knew it was her.

'Olly Owl,' she said.

'Katie Batey,' I replied.

After all those years, Olly Owl was all the prompt that I needed. Karen, even at age ten, skilfully and beautifully illustrated a cartoon strip by hand. She did this week after week for our class newspaper, also produced by hand as there was no computer assistance in those days. The newspaper was displayed on the huge school notice board. The adventures of Olly were eagerly awaited by the school pupils and me each Monday morning. Karen produced the cartoon strips at home over the weekend ready for Monday's 'publication day'. Thankfully I kept one of these as a lovely reminder and have reproduced it underneath this introduction.

Then there was Pete Smith ('Biffa'), the flying winger in one of my first football teams. He turned up at a book signing with his wife, Kath. He also turned up at my first wedding more than forty years ago, along with another boy in the team, Ranjit. As I stood with my bride on the top of the steps of Billingham Methodist Central Hall Church in an absolute downpour, these two little guys appeared soaked to the skin. They had walked the three miles plus from Norton to present us with the soggiest cardboard silver horseshoe on record. It was such a wonderful moment – they were guaranteed to be picked for the next match after the half-term break.

So many ex-pupils turned up at a book launch at Fens Primary School that I won't mention them all in case I leave anyone out. I will mention two people, however. The first is Steve Smith, an ex-member of staff who missed the book launch (he forgot!). We met up later. Steve is such a talented musician; his extraordinary renditions of Elton John's music were often played on the piano as pupils were dismissed from the hall following assemblies.

I would have given my right arm to play the piano like that. (I will resist the funny remark.)

The second was an ex-pupil, Craig Powell, another footballer, another flying winger with an eye for a goal. He rather embarrassed me by showing me a letter I had written to him when he left our school. Among other things was a reference to an outstanding display of wing play in a county-cup match away to St Peters School, Brotton, East Cleveland. Both teams had talented footballers but Craig had a fantastic game and outshone everyone on the pitch that day.

Craig, an ex-pupil at Grange School and now a governor at Fens School (the chairperson, I believe), also missed the book launch but was keen to meet up. We did meet some weeks down the line and spent an hour or more reminiscing over a cuppa and some football programmes I had made for the teams. In actual fact, I really think he wanted to challenge my choices for the team of all-time favourite players in my schools' football career.

You see, even players from the past come kicking down the proverbial manager's door. Perhaps I should have picked a squad of twenty-three players!

To dig myself out of a hole, I will try to appease Craig by saying that the team I selected was done with my heart, as one's first school is always special.

(Wow – think I may have just about got away with that!)

As I write, I have just returned from a book launch at Norton-on Tees library. Would you believe that I met more ex-pupils from almost fifty years ago. Angela Atkinson – how lovely to see her – and Rob Hill, yet another footballer. Plus Derek Graham, an old teacher mate from way back; oh, the battles we had with our respective sides on school football pitches. A lovely lad. (If only he'd known the offside rule, we might have beaten them more often! I jest.)

Derek, it was a pleasure to play any time against your

Harrowgate School.

So here is volume two. I do hope it encourages you to seek out your school chums (isn't that a lovely word?) from the past. Yes, the lovely and the loathed, the heroes and the bullies. Yes, even the bullies; you may well find that they have changed considerably with the passage of time, hopefully from the Billy/Betty Bully they were to be really grown up in every sense of the word. If they have, maybe forgiveness or apologies will be evident; if not, and you are now bigger and more powerful than them, punch them on the nose. (That is also a joke!)

Enjoy your read and if anyone would like to respond to anything in either book please contact me at (bryan. cross@hotmail.co.uk). Be warned, such are my computer skills that my reply were it strapped to the leg of an arthritic pigeon flying through fog and hounded by a bird of prey may stand a better chance of reaching you than my e-mail.

18

1 From Blackie Path to Billy North…

'C'mon lad … swing that bat like a club!'

Mr K (PE teacher)

When Thornaby on Tees was in Yorkshire, when tea was loose in a packet and when you could attend a football match without some lunatic banging a drum repeatedly, out of rhythm and in a robotic fashion, I lived a short distance from an aerodrome. Thornaby was the airfield where my dad was stationed. He was based at the local squadron, a suitable place for an air ace. Well, that's what he told me, my two brothers and my sister.

Sometime later, I discovered that he played the cornet in the RAF band. He was such a wonderfully talented player, I know that he would have been responsible for ensuring the airmen were encouraged to perform their heroic deeds. 'Bandits at 11 o'clock' or should it be 'Band Parade at 10.30.' In addition, Dad worked down a mine during the war as a reserved occupation; there may not have been danger up in the sky for him but there was danger under the ground.

*

Living in Thornaby on Tees, my first experience of school was as a pupil in the infants department at Thornaby Village School. Here I took my first faltering steps as a pupil, little realising that in about forty years' time I would be taking my large faltering steps as a head teacher.

Access for those walking to school was via the Black Path or 'Blackie Path'. Who travelled in cars in those days? There was no such thing as the school run, no concern over car parking outside the school, and I can't recall seeing any mums in their PJs! There were no safety concerns about walking down the Blackie Path to school, although I did have a pal called Ronnie whose dad said there were bears in the bushes near the path.

Having completed the journey to school, the next event was playground time. Hurrah! My favourite playground activity was leaping off the huge coal bunker, having first fastened the top button of my black gaberdine coat to transform it into a cloak as I sailed through the air before landing, often with a roll, and charging forward to save the planet from destruction. Did you know that I was a super hero? Actually, we didn't know we were super heroes at the time – that phrase came later.

Then, as I was just on the threshold of saving the world and being the saviour of the planet, the school bell would ring and it was learning the alphabet and doing 'county-ups'. Boring! But how was Miss to know? If her priorities were to get me to read and do advanced Maths, that was her choice. Me, I'd rather save the world.

All those years ago they had no idea. Two minutes earlier, Miss had been doing her head in trying to get me to read *Dick and Dora* – and I'd been leaping out of a spaceship.

They didn't realise … they still don't.

Moving on, which is wise as all my recollections of the village school and short stints in Queen's Street School and Westbury Street School (all in Thornaby) seem to be of leaping off that coal bunker. Incidentally, weren't the names of schools much more earthy and know-where-you-are names compared to the current crop? Now it's Academies, or *The* School, *The* Poplars, *The* Valley School. *The* Get-Your-Head-Kicked-In School – but we'll have a posh name to make it Sound-Good Academy .... Or, is it me?

*

My final school, as far as primary education was concerned, was Billingham North Junior School, or 'Billy North' as opposed to our great rivals 'Billy South', which, to give it the proper name, was ... oh, I'm sure you can work it out!

Here at Billy North I found my feet – literally. Well, my football education started as I found myself playing for the first eleven, actually the *only* eleven. What a proud moment it was when I was first handed my faded green footy shirt; I treasured that day.

As I was rather small the PE teacher, Mr Kitching, who was years ahead of his time in a football sense, saw me as ... well, not a target man, out-and-out striker or deep-lying centre forward (because those terms didn't exist). I was more a 'He's so tiny you don't notice him and he nips in and scores' number nine. Thus my unique role was created and I amassed a huge number of goals (four, five, even six goals in one match) by being elusive, quick and unrecognised. It was easy to sneak up on the blind side when you were as small as I was then.

Of course, it also helped having a superstar little boy called Billy Povey in the team with me. Billy, who went on to be a professional footballer, was so skilful and created goal after goal opportunity for me to add the final touch and score.

Well, someone's got to do it!

*

Football wasn't the only sporting outlet; cricket was also played in the short summer season. This was music to my ears as my dad was forever telling me that, having been born in Yorkshire, I was eligible to play for the White Rose eleven. I thought I was in. Okay, Dad, when's the first match?

Sadly I never reached those heights, although I did win the prestigious Henry Flintoft Trophy whilst playing for Castleton, a North Yorkshire village cricket team. I captained my college cricket eleven and caught the ball on the boundary for the first-ever wicket following the opening of the new pavilion at Castleton.

Howzat!

Back to Billy North. Mr Kitching was also our cricket mentor. One bright, early summer morning in May, he was standing behind the stumps barking out his instructions to our group of small boys. The boy in front of him (and in front of the stumps) was standing there rather timidly and nervously, really struggling to hit the ball. (No, it wasn't me!)

'C'mon, lad, stop messing about. Swing that bat like a club.'

The next ball was delivered. I don't know where it went; in truth no one did as we were all focused on the batsman. Morphing into a whirling dervish, the boy swung the bat as instructed. He was George slaying the Dragon; he was a *Star Wars* figure with his light sabre; he was … the little boy who smashed the bat into the forehead and trendy sunglasses of Mr Kitching.

Shock-horror as Mr K crumpled in a heap behind the

stumps, shattered shades covered in blood. The Dragon had been slain. Bleeding profusely, he was as still and silent as the rest of us. His conqueror placed his foot on Mr Kitching's chest and said, 'Was that better, Sir?'

Well, of course, I'm lying. Though only about the foot being placed on the chest. This was no laughing matter. There was our hero, Mr K, lying there now giving the faintest of moans in a dishevelled, bloody mess. What do we do?

Few ten- to eleven-year-old boys have a strategy for this sort of thing. Don't ask me why or who suggested it, but we ended up half-carrying, half-dragging the sad, sorry bundle of our PE Teacher across the grass in the direction of the playground tarmac and towards the main building.

At this point my memory fades but I'm sure our gallant band of 'paramedics' were whisked off to our classrooms and the adults took over.

Mr Kitching did not appear the next day or the next, but the following week he was back in school still bruised above the right eye and sporting a huge padded plaster.

If I recall, little cricket was played for the rest of the summer term and Mr K's image was a wee bit tarnished.

*

A few more weeks and it was goodbye primary school; the 'big' school awaited.

At this point, as with most youngsters in this country, the primary-school phase ends and school life inevitably comes to a closure in terms of the closeness and bond of class teacher and pupils. By this I mean that, in the main, it is one teacher to one class and the opportunity for bonding is much greater – well, I found it so.

That final day in class was always a difficult one to

manage. During my years in schools the final afternoon was so odd, especially with the final year in primary, the Y6 class. Often the pupils would be tearful and upset at having to leave my class. I'm not boasting about my relationship with my youngsters. I knew that for many the upset also stemmed from a deeper feeling of apprehension about the huge transition to their next school, in spite of all the wonderful phasing in that had been done by both primary and secondary establishments. It is a challenging period for the children.

As far as I was concerned, when the school gates at Billingham North School (now Pentland School) shut, my next 'brush' with primary education came many years later. In my first book I recalled the perils and pitfalls of being a trainee school teacher in college and a probationary teacher in my first year in my first school.

Incidentally, when I was a head teacher in Hartlepool two fellow head teacher colleagues, Ian and Geoff (you know who you are!), had schools close by. They were at college with me all those years ago but, to spare our blushes – and it's probably wise to do so – I will use a sporting phrase: 'What goes on, on tour, stays on tour!'

Phew Lads, that was a close call!

2 More FNJ Adventures

'Breaking in is hard to do – Trust me!'

To Mr Harvey (school caretaker)

I'm sure you recall that 1966 was a significant year, with England winning the World Cup (and me starting life as a teacher, obviously). You knew? Good, you must have bought the first book; I knew I could count on you. Have a team point.

Questions will be asked after Chapter 2; do pay attention!

What a great year to be a footballer, which I was. Thankfully I could keep up with the boys (and a girl) in my first few school teams. I was impressive; countless times I slalomed past class after class of ten and eleven year olds, brushing off their feeble challenges, flicking the ball up before volleying home past a five-feet high keeper and turning to the lonely mum laden with shopping bags as she walked by the school fence to take the applause. The cries of the players varied from 'Aw, Sir, that's not fair' to 'Great shot, Mr Cross!' from those wishing to make the school team.

Flattery will get you everywhere, son.

Quite possibly after hitting one of these 'worldies', I was so elated that I left my football boots (the ordinary black ones – the 'Joseph and the Amazing Range of Technicoloured Football Boots' had yet to be worn) in my classroom stock cupboard one Friday night. Fortunately, my memory was such in those days that I knew exactly where I'd left them. Unfortunately, my recall was on a Saturday lunchtime just after cleaning my car.

I had time to retrieve them before turning out to play for table-topping Billingham Mill Lane in the Stockton and District 'A' Division. Living close to school, I drove the one or two miles to my workplace, a dual-classroom building separate from the main block. Knowing that one of the top classroom windows did not fit securely and was of the swivel type, I reckoned that was my point of entry.

Unlocking the doors with my classroom keys was a more usual mode of entry but in those days the keys were locked securely in the school office at the end of the school day, so breaking in was my only option.

Desperate to rescue my boots (how would the team manage without their star player?), I shimmied up the drainpipe, levered open the swivel window pane of the classroom and, sitting astride the frame, was ready to drop the eight to ten feet to the floor. I was in that most uncomfortable position when I heard the chilling words, 'Good afternoon, Sir. Could we give you some assistance?'

Below me on the tarmac path stood two uniformed policemen who very kindly helped me to scramble down into the arms of the law. I explained my situation and I don't think they really believed me. Just as an 'X' written as a signature is pretty neutral, saying 'I'm Mr Cross' has a kind of made-up name ring to it. Well, they must have thought so.

Perhaps my clothes didn't help: paint-stained tracksuit, worn, down-at-heel shoes – my clean-the-car gear. Whatever the reason, they didn't believe me.

'Mr Harvey's the school caretaker. His house is near the entrance to the drive. You can ask him to verify who I am.'

I said this as I was being handcuffed and manhandled down to Mr Harvey's house with me shouting at them, 'You'll never pin this on me, cop.' (This is not true but a bit of fiction as a result of watching far too many police drama series on television.)

In actual fact, we walked calmly down the drive to the caretaker's house. Indeed, I could have sprinted clear of them both but thought better of it.

Proceeding towards the door in a northerly direction ... (you see, straight from a copper's notebook) we knocked on Mr Harvey's door. He appeared immediately. Now I hadn't been at the school overlong but Mr Harvey knew me well – too well. I often left the school late after football practices when he was locking up at six o'clock or thereabouts. Maybe this was the reason he reacted as he did. Who knows? I often delayed his locking up so perhaps this was payback time.

He looked at me blankly. 'Who is this supposed to be?'

'Mr Harvey, it's me. Mr Cross, the football teacher.'

He still looked puzzled.

One of the policemen turned away then they all started laughing. Whether Mr H. had given them a crafty wink I don't know but, as my white face turned bright red, one of the policemen said sternly, 'I'll leave the culprit with you.'

After suitable explanations Mr Harvey said, 'I'll get the classroom keys.'

What a pre-match routine. It could have been the earliest red card in the history of the game of football.

Of course I got my boots, played a great game on the afternoon and scored two goals. Get in!

It could have been that the police officers sharpened my senses or maybe it was the elation of knowing that, if

I could escape the long arm of the law, I could escape the long legs of the opposition's defence.

Fair play to Mr Harvey, the episode was never mentioned to anyone as far as I know. Certainly I cannot recall muttering or sniggering behind my back by any member of staff at my attempted break-in. But, as you may have read in my first book, (see, I'm still checking on your reading habits) my teaching colleagues were 'proper' teachers in those days and such gossip would never have entered their heads ... thankfully.

Oh, before I leave this section did I mention that my team won the Stockton and District 'A' Division league? I've got the medal at home.

*

Mentioning reading habits, getting good reading material into the hands of the children in the school and the children in my class was always a priority. A time for reading was a daily routine with my pupils and, I assume, all the other classes. Grouped in threes, fours or fives according to reading ability, this was a new pattern to adapt to when I had my own class.

On teaching practice before I qualified, tutors carrying out observations didn't want to (or didn't *seem* to want to – I could be wrong) see you sit listening to children reading; they wanted to see you doing 'real' teaching, all singing-and-dancing performances...

'Now, children, this is my rendition of the Roald Dahl book *Charlie and the Chocolate Factory,* with suitable facial expressions and a different voice for each character. At the same time, I will be hollowing out a marrow with my feet, and in our Science lesson this afternoon we will learn how to light the whole of our school with three

AAA batteries and the class hamster.' (Get outta here!)

Yes, the class reading groups. Most of the time I sat in with groups but occasionally I just sat and read suitable books and magazines at my desk. Just as I invited individual children in the groups to explain what they were reading, I invited them to ask me about the stuff I was reading. I was very selective in my material (I left my *Beano* annual at home). My thinking was to encourage them to develop into adult readers as I'm sure not too many of them saw their parents as avid readers, or readers at all. It was hardly cutting-edge teaching but I was keen to give my pupils the 'passport' that learning to read provides to further – indeed any – studies.

To establish these reading groups, children were tested regularly to establish their reading ages. We used the Schonell Reading Tests printed on cards, a series of five words, line after line, which were deemed increasingly difficult to read as you moved down the page.

Truly, I can still remember them now:

tree little egg milk book
school sit frog playing bun
picture think summer people
something etc. etc.

In actual fact, I can remember them as clearly as my favourite football team line-up from about the same time. For example, the 'Boro' (Middlesbrough FC) formation: starting in goal Ugolini, Bell, Stonehouse, Harris, Dicks, Yeoman … and so on. Considering the disappointments of MFC during my early teaching years, I think *tree, little, egg, milk, book* would have defended the goal much better. Sorry, boys.

Imagine forty-eight children with five to ten minutes

for each one to read the test card and for me to record the results and establish the reading ages and groupings... You do the maths. It took a long, long time. There were no parent helpers and no teaching assistants, and testing was done every few weeks.

Thus, I often arrived at school early in the morning. Thirty to forty minutes before the 9am hand bell, I invited children to come into class from the yard to do the test. Pupils were most willing on cold frosty mornings; then they needed no invitation, in fact they were queueing up to read. Then, with the '*tree, little, egg...*' words ringing in my ears, it would be assembly time at 9am.

One of the assembly songs I remember went as follows – please sing along if you remember the tune:

Glad that I live am I
That the sky is blue
Glad for the country lanes
And the fall of dew
After the sun the rain
After the rain the sun
This is the way of life
Till the day be done.

Standing at the side of the rows of cross-legged children who were sitting on the floor, I would sing along. However, such was the impact of the reading test words that my sung words, without realising it, on occasions would morph into:

Glad that I live am I
That the sky is blue
Tree, little, egg, milk, book
And the fall of dew
After the sun the rain

After the rain the sun
This is the way of life
School, sit, frog, playing, bun!

*

At times, assemblies were brightened up by guests. One in particular was a huge West Indian musician who may have been called Constantine. He played a guitar with a calypso beat and sang some folk songs and hymns.

To say that his initial appearance was dramatic is an understatement. It was a cold, damp morning and my reading testing was on hold in spite of the appetite for reading by the clamouring children, faces pressed up against the classroom window. I was seeking warmth myself and attempting to close in on the open coal fire blazing away in the small, cramped staff room at the top of the stairs above the school office.

The 'proper' teachers, as I'm sure I will always call them, were there, one puffing on a pipe, the ladies discussing matters of the day, all in their usual chairs. Suddenly the door burst open to Jamaican sunshine and there stood this large black man, flashing white teeth, an orange jacket and a red, woolly, bobble hat atop his thick, black fuzzy hair.

'Is dis da Frederick Nattrass School?'

The drab greyness of the staff room was lit up by his West Indian frame filling the door space. Total shock from staff as this cheerful, charming and colourful Constantine fellow announced his arrival. Eventually, as staff adjusted to this shock to their systems, we engaged with him, shared a cuppa and enjoyed this lovely, friendly visitor.

He was a big hit with the children during the assembly and was a talking point for days. Remember that this was the 1960s and very few of our children had seen a live black man, certainly not one as colourful and charismatic as Constantine. The children loved him and I remember his staff-room appearance and the looks on the faces of staff as he burst in. Their faces, open-mouthed, were a joy to behold. Would that I had captured the scene on camera.

Guppy fish at feeding time.

No, I'm not being disrespectful, but it was oh so funny. I may well have worn a guppy fish expression too!

3 Keep it in the Family…

'Well, Mr Clark, some of our parents do get carried away…'

Mr C (Cross) to Mr C (Boss)

It was the way he said it: 'My big brother wants to see you.' Just a hint of threat – and when he followed up with the word… 'Tonight!'

I took a deep swallow. 'Good, I'm looking forward to seeing him,' I replied, being less than honest.

A pupil in my first class, Kevin (it's not his real name, of course – I'm not stupid), was not always the most calm and well-behaved young man. I hoped that his brother was.

The day passed by and at four o'clock parents came and the children departed. I waited and waited for big brother. At about 4.30 I checked the path toward the classroom, not for the first time. In the distance, some hundred yards away (we had not gone metric then), the figure of a man appeared. I blanched: he was big, with wide shoulders, long legs and a shaven head.

For some reason, I thought I would walk towards him and greet him. How did I know it was him? I just knew!

We walked slowly towards each other. I felt like a gun-fighter at the OK Corral. If you've seen Clint Eastwood movies or the film *High Noon,* you may be able to picture the scene. Slowly, under the blazing sun, we moved closer and faced each other down.

He looked about nineteen or twenty years of age but he was fully grown – a big lad!

'Are you Kevin's teacher?' he growled.

'Yes,' I replied in the strongest macho voice possible although in actual fact it may have been a high-pitched, squeak.

'Well, I hope you're looking after him and he's alright.' Then he turned and walked away.

'Nice to meet you,' I said, as he moved off.

That was it.

Survived: our 'interview' was over. That went quite well, I thought.

I think going to meet him outside the classroom was key; going inside would possibly have been a greater challenge for him and could well have caused tension and aggression. After all, it did just that for his younger brother Kevin.

Job done.

All those years ago; it seems a nothing kind of thing now but then I was a 'rookie' teacher. Let's say I was relieved when it was over.

The following day I had a word first thing with Kevin as the class lined up in the yard after morning bell. 'Nice to see your brother last night, Kevin,' I said.

I expected him to reply with, 'He said you were a frightfully, splendid chap.' In fact, he seemed to mutter something under his breath.

I took it no further.

*

Not only were my pupils' families involved in school life but my own family was too. My nephew, David, was in my first class, which was an astute move by Mr Clark, the headmaster.

My sister-in-law thought so too. 'Don't worry, Bryan, he'll be as good as gold. He won't let the family down, certainly not you as his uncle. Your brother Arthur and I will see to that!'

Well, David was as good as gold and no one worked harder that first year. His scores proved it; indeed, in the class exams he gained the highest score. Rather embarrassing in a way because I'm sure some folk thought it was fixed. It wasn't.

My first school team was captained by another nephew, Alan. He was another outstanding footballer. The boys in the team chose him to lead the side so who was I to argue?

Then there was my dad, bless him. I think, in terms of anger management (or lack of – you will recall, an incident in Book 1) it was football that, in the main, caused one or two problems.

Let me say that Dad was a lovely man, kind and caring. He was always a big Middlesbrough FC supporter; the Boro was 'his' team. He was quite vocal in his support, yet not once did I hear him swear or use improper language. Dad had a stock phrase, when a forward player was spoken of as 'dangerous' near goal. Whether on the home or away side, Dad would always reply, 'Who? Him? Dangerous? He couldn't be dangerous with a gun!' That always made me laugh

Permit me to digress on this subject of shouting out at football matches. In my younger days, the individual cries of football supporters were funny and, apart from racist comments (and I heard few, if any at all, thank goodness), were generally good humoured. Certainly they were a far cry from the banal chants heard from great swathes of supporters today such as: 'We are (*insert any manager bloke's name*) Red and White, or Blue and Orange (*or any garish colour worn nowadays*) Army!'

Now there's nothing wrong with the chant as such, but when it's repeated ad nauseam, ten to fifteen minutes at a time, I lose the will to live. It makes me expect a tribal war dance in the middle of the pitch and an altar set up with the team mascot sacrificed with a dagger through the heart. I wish – don't get me started on team mascots.

Do these chanting people manage to switch off when they go back home? The sound must echo through their skull for days. How they manage to sleep beats me.

Then, of course, there's the obscene chanting. What have we come to?

One of the funniest individual shouts I've ever heard referred to the centre forward (sorry 'striker' or 'front-man') whose heading ability was less than perfect: 'He's got a head like a threepenny bit.' For younger readers, a threepenny bit was a brass, bronze-coloured coin with twelve sides. I suppose an alternative cry could have been: 'He's got a head like a dodecagonal,' but somehow that just doesn't seem to cut the mustard.

So, back to Dad. As a great football enthusiast, he followed me in all matters of sport in all the football teams I played for, both school and adult. He also followed the teams I coached in schools.

I remember one match in particular. It was a cup game against a team in Thornaby. At the half-time interval the score was 0–0 and stayed that way till a few minutes before what should have been the final whistle. Another five minutes played; surely it was time but no, the game continued. As a young teacher, I didn't want to shout out 'Hey, ref, time's up!' but kept trying to point out as politely as possible by making remarks to my boys such as, 'Keep going lads only a minute to go' or 'Nearly time for the whistle boys!'

The referee was an experienced teacher but his sense of time was woeful (I am being kind). On and on the game continued until the opposing team scored after what must have been ten more minutes of the allotted time. The boys in my team were shattered and conceded two more goals in the extra minutes before the final whistle blew.

My dad was seething and remarked quite loudly how disappointed he was with the ref and the length of the second half. He was right; it had been grossly unfair.

As the teams were getting changed after the game, the teacher in question mentioned that he had had a problem with his watch. I'll say he did!

There is always a difficulty with refereeing your own team. When I was doing so, I tended to err on the side of the other team, so much so that my school team preferred it when they were playing away. But not this particular day.

In the middle of the following week, my head teacher, Mr Clark, asked me to have a word with him in his office. He was also a keen football man; a pupil from one of his former schools went on to become an England international goalkeeper – I believe it was Hopkinson or Hodgkinson, who played for one of the Sheffield teams. Mr Clark often came to watch our school games. How I wish he had attended this one.

He had received a letter of complaint from the head of the school in Thornaby about one of our parents complaining about their referee. What could I say other than, 'Well, Mr Clark, some of our parents do get carried away.' He probably thought I was referring to the parents of our players; little did he realise that I was referring to my own dad.

To be fair, my dad and Mr Clark got on well. Indeed, I recall Dad joining us for a trip to Wembley Stadium for a schoolboys' international match and they got on famously. If Mr Clark had known the true circumstances of the game against Thornaby, he would have realised Dad was quite justified in getting hot under the collar.

Whatever the reasoning, I was glad when I was out of the office.

*

Sometimes my officiating in football matches was questioned. Never, I hear you say? Oh yes!

One day our centre forward, Nicky, was up-ended in the penalty area as a result of a clumsy challenge by the opposition defender. Nicky, a slightly built boy, fell rather heavily to the ground. I awarded the spot kick, as the fall certainly denied Nicky a certain goal, but before it was taken a shout and scream heralded the arrival of our Number 9's mum.

She came charging across the field with toddler in pushchair. 'That's ridiculous, Mr Cross, send him off!' She turned to her son and asked, 'Are you alright, love?'

Then she turned to the boy who had committed the foul. 'You ought to be ashamed of yourself, you bully.'

Eventually she calmed down, order was restored and the game continued.

What a difference it would make if this were allowed in premiership football, if mums could enter the field of play and challenge the behaviour of players. 'Get up, you cheat, that was a dive! My (*insert name of any pro footballer*) never touched you! Did you, son?'

Wow! *Match of the Day* would never be the same.

*

It meant such a lot for children to get into the school team. I like to think that as a team we did things in the right way, we played in the right way,.

I have seen school teams with outstanding individuals where the general idea seemed to be give the ball to the star player so he could go past everyone, score heaps of goals and that's it, game over.

Really? Is that what team playing is about?

We had some very good individual players in all the school teams I was responsible for but, if we were to win games and trophies by playing as though one individual mattered more than anyone else, I would have been doing all of them a disservice, especially the star.

If it had not been for one of these stars on an opposing team, we would have won the Stockton Schools League with a team from my first school. The star concerned scored the equalising goal and denied us a victory that would have given us the points to win the trophy. Then, to rub in the proverbial salt, after the match their sports teacher told me how this particular star player shouldn't really have been playing as his behaviour in school that day had been appalling.

He went on to say, 'We couldn't leave him out. You see how good he is.'

No comment!

It was hardly the Premiership or the European Cup title we were going for, but it meant as much to our lads and it left me with a sour taste in my mouth. I felt this was, in a very minor way, the attitude that develops with sporting 'superstars'; they feel that they are untouchable, and discipline and justice does not apply in the same way to them.

One little boy, who was mad keen to be in the team, frequently pestered me to play. I won't mention his name but his initials were BM and he did eventually play one or two games. For effort and enthusiasm, he was outstanding. Here is a little verse I have written dedicated to all those boys desperate to be 'in the team':

Please, Sir, can I be captain and play a midfield role?
I'll make our school team famous.
Well – can I play in goal?
I'll be the bravest keeper and dive on muddied knees.
No one will ever score past me.
Alright, Sir, but…
Pleeease.
Maybe you think a striker, I've got a great right foot,
Up front I'd stick them in the net…
I'm not too fast, Sir,
But…
So, if I'm slow and rather fat and height's a thing I lack,
Perhaps I'll wear the 2 or 3 and play as full back.
There's just no chance…
Oh, just a sub… Well … okay, Sir, that's fine.
Yes, I'll be there on Saturday
Oranges half-time!

*

And finally, although it's nothing to do with families, an incident that I thought was so amusing that I ought to tell you before leaving my Frederick Nattrass' days.

We often took school trips to London, sometimes sightseeing in the capital, sometimes to watch the schoolboy international football games at Wembley Stadium and, on occasion, a combination of both.

On one such excursion we were in Trafalgar Square. The sun was shining and the birds were singing, except for the pigeons who were busy feasting on corn sold in small pots to the visitors. This was fine but not if you had an aversion to our feathered friends. One of our teachers, Mr G, had such an aversion. He politely warned our pupils not to feed the birds.

Sadly, one of our children did not hear this instruction and returned to the group with his pot of bird seed. Mr G was not pleased and called the young man to stand in front of him.

'Didn't you hear what I said, son?' Mr G remarked loudly to the offending pupil.

'No, Sir, sorry, Sir,' replied the boy.

'Get rid of it!' bawled Mr G.

Now Mr G could well have expected this young man to walk calmly over to the nearest litter bin and deposit his purchase of bird seed safely into the refuse container. He thought wrongly.

Acting exactly as advised, the boy threw the bird seed on the floor. The whole of the contents. What an obedient little fellow.

The floor was directly beneath Mr G's brown shoes, which were soon covered in scores of pigeons. So, it seemed, was the rest of Mr G's person.

Back at the hotel that night, Mr G asked me to supervise the boys in their rooms. He sought a darkened room in which to lie down.

4 The Great Outdoors...

'Can ye no hear the pipes...'

Mr Cameron, 'Bagpiper'

On moving to Hartlepool, not only did I have to learn the language (this is an attempt at being funny... although 'My dad *werks* at the *werks*' is pretty universal around these parts of the North East) but also the geography of the town. In truth, I was well guided by staff, almost all of whom were Hartlepudlians. Isn't that a terrific name – and I'm not joking. It is.

Hartlepool was a sizeable place and yet everyone on the staff seemed to have links of a sort with everyone in the town.

Don't make fun of Charlie, the man who runs the off licence in York Road, for the chances are that the teacher in next door's classroom has an uncle who married a waitress who has an aunty whose father put the tops on the beer bottles in Cameron's Brewery who used to go fishing off the Headland with Charlie's stepbrother.

Well, you can't be too careful.

As well as enjoying this new environment, I had the opportunity to share upwards of a week, Friday to Friday, in the great outdoors, namely at Carlton Outdoor Centre. Located in the village of Carlton-in-Cleveland, about two or three miles from the market town of Stokesley, it provided a welcome break from the school classroom for most of the pupils in the Hartlepool Primary Schools. The children enjoyed their time there too.

Originally bequeathed to the children of West Hartlepool, grandparents, parents and children have been clambering up to the top of Pin Point, the Hartlepudlians' Everest, for many years. It's always been a 'must do' outing for local schools.

As I write a dear friend, Roger Smith, has clocked up a glorious fifty years' service taking children from Stranton Primary School to Carlton Outdoor Centre. Fittingly, he was presented with a silver salver to mark the occasion and an annual award has been initiated within the school to recognise his achievement. Well done, Roger, I believe the local hostelry, The Blackwell Ox, is also preparing to honour him in some small way … I can't think why!

Incidentally, it was the same Roger who, thanks to his snoring, caused me great distress. I had to move my mattress to the floor of the corridor outside our leaders' room to avoid sound waves of seismic proportions. The noise was still quite audible but just about bearable, though rumour has it that St Botolph's Church bells were almost rung to warn villagers of the impending tremors of an earthquake.

Of course I forgive you, Roger; in fact, the phrase 'take up your bed and walk' from the Bible has become even more meaningful to me thanks to your night-time utterances.

*

The logo on the cover of this book belongs to FOCCA, the Friends of Carlton Camp Association. FOCCA is a charity which was formed in 2014 by a group of teachers, local businessmen, ex-head teachers and individuals who are passionate about the legacy of Carlton Camp, now known as Carlton Adventure. The charity was formed with the aim of ensuring that all children, especially the most underprivileged, are given the opportunity to experience life in the great outdoors. Carlton itself is a special place for all the 'FOCCers', who tirelessly raise money to fund trips to the centre for deprived children and also to ensure that Carlton is maintained, supported and has a lasting legacy. You can visit the website www.friendsofcarltoncamp.co.uk for more information or to help raise funds for this excellent local charity.

For many weeks I absented myself from my Hartlepool schools, Fens and Grange, to spend a rewarding time with our children and staff at Carlton Outdoor Centre, plus the schools with whom we shared the week. They were such wonderful times; they were challenging for the children as they gained independence, learned to live and share together, and often provided a platform for discovering the joy and wonder of the countryside.

Understandably, not all staff put themselves forward for the week away at Carlton because it was certainly a challenge for them too. On reflection, it was a big responsibility but it was also such a pleasure to see children blossom into new patterns of life.

Of course, for teachers a further problem of sleep deprivation was a paramount issue, as I will explain later.

At times some schools would take the full complement of seventy-two children plus staff, but in the main they shared their time with another school, with each school taking thirty-six pupils. Things have changed over the years and now all Cleveland Primary schools are eligible to take an allocation. After that 'furry Frenchie spy incident' you would have thought they would have learned their lesson. Huh, 'foreigners'!

But no: typical Hartlepool people, forgiving and kind.

Sharing with other schools was quite a challenge. Sharing with people they did not know at the meal table, in dormitories during 'free time' – all these things were difficult but the staff managed quite well. The children were no trouble; they were brilliant.

The experience for adults and children was wonderful. At the end of the full week, friendships had often been forged that would last a long time. Such was the joy of a week at Carlton. Indeed, together with the three main schools I have worked at, Carlton Outdoor Centre plus Tilery and Oxbridge Schools (where I helped out with a wee bit of supply teaching in my twilight years) were my 'adopted' schools. Children and staff alike were always a joy, and I always felt welcome and happy there.

*

Characters were far more in evidence when living the outdoor life. The children were all similarly clad, kitted out in cagoules and boots, with the array of 'bobble hats' being the only distinguishing feature.

The staff were another matter.

Enter Mr I-Was-Not-Cut-out-for-Walking-and-I-Don't-Know-Why-I-Came-Away-for-the-Week, a member of staff with a visiting school.

Mr (let's call him Smith – and no, it wasn't Roger) Smith surprised us all when he joined the assembly point in front of the main building. Everyone else was dressed in standard walking gear but Mr Smith was wearing a light gaberdine coat, highly polished brogue shoes and carrying a walking stick. Now, we were only going for a short walk, not exactly climbing the north face of the Eiger, but for goodness' sake, man, make an effort!

I didn't expect a Bear Grylls costume but, golly gumdrops, should someone tell him?

In his defence, he was a lovely chap and a joy to be with throughout the week. Thanks to the outdoor centre costumiers who found him some appropriate clothing, he did eventually blend in with us in terms of looking the part.

*

Children also left a lasting impression, not just as individuals but in their groups. One particular week we took a party that including a ten-year-old girl whose mam had died just over a week before we travelled. As party leader, I was unsure whether this was a good thing for the group as a whole but the family were happy for her to attend. The brave young lady wanted to come along and my female colleague, who was with the group of girls in their dormitory, was strong and caring enough to take up the challenge.

The whole group were absolutely wonderful and, although there were times that were a bit tricky, all in all I was so proud of the whole group.

Over the years, children have often shown a care, understanding and resilience that has amazed me and this was certainly one of those occasions.

Then there was a young lady whom I met up with recently who jogged my memory in terms of a 'Tetley Tea Bag' dance. Those of you advanced in years may recall the television advert – not how we performed it. Thanks to a splendid piece of choreography by yours truly, the dance was performed by the children near the trig point on the top of Pin Point.

Dawn P (I will not give her full name for fear of embarrassment) came away from her week at Carlton with this as her main memory. I laugh in the face of *Strictly Come Dancing*!

You must admit that I gave these children a truly well-rounded education. I'm sure Dawn has had many occasions to perform this dance with skill in her adult life, with work colleagues, family and friends. No doubt she impressed them all and her career advanced three-fold; opportunities came in abundance thanks to this school-teacher initiated gift.

Yes, when children left our school, they were well equipped for the rigours of adulthood.

Outdoor activities and environmental studies ... y'can't beat them.

*

This is a good time to introduce Ricky, a young man who attended with his 'special' school, which had boys and girls with varying disabilities.

Ricky was without full upper limbs – and what a superstar he was. Full of life and mischievous fun – what a handful! The boys in our dorm watched in awe as he went about his daily tasks and were open-mouthed when he got changed in the evening, thanks to his special school mates helping him off with his trousers and on with his pyjama bottoms.

In a similar vein, two of our young ladies (in the dining hall, the pattern was that two girls sat at the four-seater table with two boys from the special school) were amazed as Ricky kicked off his flip-flops during their first breakfast meal together, lifted a foot on the table, held a breakfast cereal bar with his toes and started eating.

Come the end of the week and the two girls from our school didn't bat an eyelid at Ricky's table routines. All four of them chatted away; this is what children do and I thought it was so wonderful. So wonderful that, as I'm writing this, I'm wondering if this really did happen those many years ago. But yes, my friends, it truly did and I'm a better person for seeing it.

It was the best week away I've ever had with any group of children.

*

Remember that I mentioned sleep deprivation earlier? Well, a person suffering such a fate was Mr Cameron, my fellow member of staff. I had been on numerous Carlton trips and was aware of first-night difficulties in getting the pupils to sleep because they were experiencing a combination of excitement, energy and missing home. To my friend Mr C (a 'virgin' Carlton Camper) it was a sobering experience and I'm afraid he suffered badly, being disturbed repeatedly from his slumber the first night he was away.

In seeking to inflict a bit of retribution, he decided it would be 'payback' time later in the week. Four days later, around midnight when the boys were exhausted and sleeping soundly due to the walks and outdoor exercise, Mr C stood in the middle of the boys' dorm with a hunting horn. (Did I tell you that Mr C was a peripatetic teacher of brass instruments and had special permission to share the week with us?)

He decided it was a suitable time for a practice. I leave you to imagine the chaos.

Boys dorm – 1; Mr C – 1

I'm saying little else, other than that the remaining night-time sleeps were soundless.

The slumber traumas did not dampen Mr C's enthusiasm and fun; in fact, the children thought he was great to be with because of his escapades and sense of adventure. This was exemplified by the Old Coach Road incident.

Close by the Centre is Busby Hall and leading from the hall to the road is a cart track called the Old Coach Road. It is steeped in legend and ghostly stories; the children were told many tales at the campfire sing-songs about the Grey Lady, a ghost who patrols this road at night. Whooo!

Over the years children had been taken on night walks along this road and it was a good bit of fun. As far as I know, none of the children in groups I had taken along there had been whisked away. That's quite sad really; some of the less-than-charming children I encountered from time to time would have given the Grey Lady a run for her money. In fact, she could well have given up spooking people and entered a nunnery!

So back to the plot…

Off we go again on a night-time walk along the Old Coach Road. Mr Cameron had gone back home to Teesside for the evening for a break – so we thought.

Plodding along the road with our torches, we were chatting away discussing Grey Ladies and the fun of the week away. Suddenly, in the silence of the starry night, there was a wailing sound and a dark figure stepped out from behind a hedge some hundred yards in front of us. It approached, more visible under the moonlit sky. It was a tall man dressed in a kilt, sporran and additional Scots' garb, playing the bagpipes. It was a pretty scary apparition but I knew who it was and I guess most of the children did, too.

'It's the ghostly Scotsman,' I said. 'He's a very good friend of Mrs Grey Lady.'

Eventually we met up and everyone had a good laugh with Mr C. He had taken the trouble to go home get changed to provide us with a lot of fun and enjoyment. What a character!

Homesick, our children? No chance. There was never a dull moment and they didn't have time to dwell on things at home, not with our staff.

*

In case you are thinking that taking the children to Carlton was just for fun, may I say the benefits as a whole were a bit more than that. But I'm not going to 'sell' Carlton, or indeed any outdoor residential centres. When we were there we did our educational studies and classroom work in a different context, but bringing children together in schools and educational centres/outdoor centres is not filling up empty vessels. I am reminded of a university student who allegedly tore up his degree certificate and sent it back to his university with a note saying: 'You taught me how to earn a living but you never taught me how to live.'

In my mind we have a duty to address the way children interact with each other and with adults, to show respect, to care, to love, to accept there will be highs and lows in life and to deal with them accordingly.

I'll stop there. I'm getting a bit 'preachy' and 'teachery' and that's not the purpose of this book. Sorry!

*

Before I step back into the safety and sanctuary of the classroom, so to speak, here is a lovely little Carlton story – plus one from another Outdoor Centre that could have had a much worse ending.

It was during a trip with Fens school children from my Y6 class. We were walking down the drive at the centre with our cases and bags to the waiting bus. I had acquired a stick on one of our walks at the beginning of the week and had taken it out with me every day. It was a struggle to carry my case and bags with my stick under my arm; finding it difficult to hang onto, I threw it over the high hedge skirting the path and into the farmer's field.

I thought nothing more about it until a few months down the line. It was the final day of the school year and my class were leaving for a new school. Children and parents were always so kind on the final day, not only giving farewell presents but often mums coming in to say thanks.

One girl (I'm so annoyed I can't recall her name but, if she is reading this, please get in touch) went out of the classroom, met her mum in the corridor and came back clutching 'my stick'. The one I had thrown over the hedge. It was a bit different: it had been smoothed and polished and had a little brass plate about the size of the side of a matchbox with the words: *To Mr Cross, thanks for Carlton*.

It was such a lovely, unusual surprise and perhaps the nicest thing I have ever been given by a pupil who was leaving my school. Apparently, all those weeks earlier at Carlton, she had moved to the back of the crocodile line of children, asked permission to pick up the stick, sneaked it aboard the bus and her dad had done it up. What a thoughtful thing to do.

Sadly, over the years the stick broke having been so well used, but I retrieved the little brass plate and it is there to this day somewhere amongst my teaching memorabilia.

Ah, happy, happy memories!

*

Before I close this chapter there is yet another memory that I will record, having been reminded of this in a talk I was invited to do at Norton-on-Tees library. This was quite close to my first school, Frederick Nattrass Juniors. Inevitably ex-pupils turned up (you can't get rid of 'em!) and reminded me that I had also done a few outdoor weeks away with them.

As far as I can recall, no one at the school had taken groups of children away for a week to an outdoor camp before that. It is a challenge for all concerned to be whisked away from mams and dads and families for a week, especially for primary-aged children. I can understand for all sorts of reasons why many staff decline to do it but I was prepared to stick my head above the parapet, as it were. As you may have gathered, 'sticking my head over the parapet' seemed to figure quite a lot in my teaching career.

'What? Go away for a week with little… (please insert the name of any child that may have been a little difficult)? It's bad enough coping with him/her from nine till four.'

I know, I know. Certainly it is a responsibility, as this tale will show.

The residential centre was called Dukeshouse Wood and was situated a few miles from Hexham in Northumberland. We were two or three days into the week and the children were well into all the activities, walking in forests, along Hadrian's Wall, visiting the abbey at Hexham…

There were no particular concerns and children from a

52

mix of schools, including secondary, were getting along fine. It was towards lunchtime and we were getting ready for lunch in the dining hall. We were involved in a rare 'in camp' activity – it was rare because we were normally away from the centre at lunchtimes.

The youngsters were assembling near the dining hall area when one of the centre mini-buses came trundling along the drive and stopped near the reception building. Two boys stepped out with suitcases. Were my eyes deceiving me? No, they were not: they were two of our boys.

I walked them along to my room and they told their tale. Both lads (probably the toughest of the group) had been missing their mams so much they decided to do a runner. Grabbing their cases, which had been in a locked cupboard (they had seen a staff member getting some cleaning materials, nipped in and grabbed their two cases – well, a case and a hold-all) – they shoved them under their bunks. They stuffed all their gear into them and, at the start of the short free-time break before lunch, walked out of the centre.

How they managed to do this without being spotted I will never know. Fortunately, one of the centre staff who was returning up the road in the mini-bus from Hexham had seen these two boys walking down the road and returned them to base.

Both of them sat there on my bed in tears. I gave them my homesickness talk and explained how foolish they were leaving on their own and the danger they could have been in. They were hoping to get on the train at the station and head off back to Teesside. Neither of them had any money and they were walking down a very busy road – the possible consequences of their actions were frightening.

I'm sure that within a few minutes of being in the dining hall we would have realised that two of our group were missing and the 'manhunt' would have been on. But, as a young teacher, it was a painful lesson in the responsibilities of taking children away from their home environment.

The boys finished off the week but my eyes were on them like a hawk just in case they fancied a repeat performance. In actual fact, I think they were a bit concerned that their street cred had been blown and that their mates might have seen them in tears. Certainly they were the least obvious candidates to have broken down in tears. For me, it was another steep learning curve and a reminder to take nothing for granted in terms of assuming you know how children will react.

Somehow I don't think they boasted to their pals of their escapade; indeed, I doubt if many of the group knew about it. Maybe their mindset was that if they spoke of it Sir might tell about them being 'cry-babies'.

Who knows?

5 The Long and Winding Road…

'By gum, lad, you're right – it is a goat!'

A Westerdale Farmer

So, back to the school and classrooms in Hartlepool. During my time there, I moved house from Stockton-on-Tees and lived in Castleton, a lovely village situated on the North Yorkshire Moors. It was quite a journey to and from school, as you can imagine, but gave me time to prepare mentally for the day ahead and to wind down from the day that had been.

There was certainly a need to wind down after the hectic school days. On one occasion, when we were preparing for a school concert, we had hired some huge theatre lights to illuminate the stage. These were massive, heavy lights with powerful beams. Sadly, during the adjustment of the lighting, one of the teachers received quite a severe electric shock and the lights fell with a crash onto the dining-room tables in the school hall. Maybe we should have left it to the professionals but staff always had energy, enthusiasm and innovative ideas to try these tasks themselves.

Then there was the conker championship, an annual event we held in the autumn term. Children competed in preliminary heats in the classrooms under staff supervision before the grand final in the hall. We arranged a system of banked seating with chairs, benches and stage blocks, and the 'conker gladiators' competed in this arena in the semis and the final of this prestigious competition. Held after school, we had up to a hundred pupils watching the competitors. The winner walked off with the prize: same award, year after year, a Ladybird book, *William the Conqueror*. What else?

Of course, today conkers are banned in schools, unless children are wearing industrial goggles and gardening gloves.

Good old days... I'll say!

*

So, the journey to Hartlepool was quite a drive each day and not always without incident. I drove from Castleton to Hartlepool, more often than not via the tiny villages of Commondale and Kildale, before reaching the market town of Stokesley, dodging tractors, trailers, sheep (always the sheep) and an assortment of wild creatures. There were pheasants and grouse by the score, the twisting and turning lapwings. At certain times of the year, my journey was enhanced by a background carpet of vivid purple heather and ling. All this after walking my Labrador 'Barny' (an anagram of ... guess who?) on the moortops before school each morning. One of the teachers was under the impression that Barny was my son. She was rather relieved when she discovered he was a dog.

In addition to these fascinating creatures, there was once a goat...

Driving to school one morning and going across the moors above Westerdale village, I spied in the distance the white bedraggled figure of a goat. There was drizzle in the air and the goat was flopped at the side of the narrow moorland road. I was driving a rather old banger of a car – how it managed the daily trip I will never know. Somehow I always seem to drive this type of motor vehicle.

Why I decided to pull over near the poor unfortunate creature I cannot tell. Perhaps you will have gathered by now that I often do foolhardy, impulsive things. I opened the back door of the car and the goat happily leapt on to the back seat. Certainly Billy (well, have you got a better name?) couldn't damage the upholstery. The front passenger seat, if I recall, was under repair and had a large strip of wide black tape just under the head rest.

Turning around, I noticed a pile of exercise books from my class which I had taken home for marking. To my horror, Billy took an instant fancy to them and munched his way through a number of them before I dropped him off in Westerdale village. What an excuse for children not finishing their work.

'Well I did complete it, Sir, but the page was eaten by a goat!'

I was under the impression that only wet dogs shook themselves. While I am not sure about the rest of the animal kingdom, I can assure you that goats also do this activity. My white shirt could testify to this as it was spotted with muddy moisture from the goat!

Stopping the car in the high street in Westerdale village I viewed my options. A light was on in the second cottage in the row of terraced cottages that make up the start of the housing on the turn off from Castleton. Smoke was coming from the chimney, a sign that someone may have started the day.

Leaving the car and pushing open the wooden gate at the end of the path to the cottage, I knocked at the door. I was greeted eventually by an old farmer. He was wearing wellies and an old raincoat, and had a flat cap on his head, so I assumed he wasn't a chartered accountant.

'Aye, lad?'

'Well, I've got a goat in the back seat of my car. It's worn out. Could you look after it?'

He didn't say yes and he didn't say no but invited me into his cottage. He walked over to a large stove and took a huge boiling kettle off the hob. 'Are you sure it's not a sheep, lad?'

'No, it's a goat. I know the difference.'

He looked dubious; perhaps it was my mud-spattered white shirt and West Hartlepool Rugby Club tie. Going to the back door, he took a few lengths of bailer twine and said, 'Okay, let's have a see.'

Nearing the car, he gripped the cuff of his coat, used it to wipe the back window and peered in. 'By gum. You're right, lad, it is a goat!'

'I told you it was a goat,' I said, grateful now that I'd studied that *I-Spy Country Animals* book.

'Right, let's have it out,' the farmer said. He opened the back door of the car, effortlessly tied the twine around the goat's neck and led it up the path.

As Mr Farmer and Billy disappeared up the path I called out, 'See y'later.'

Sitting in the mud-spattered car, half-eaten books on the back seat, I thought what a way to start a school day!

Needless to say, my class loved the story and, along with the evidence of the chewed-up books, it kept them amused for the whole of the morning.

What happened to the goat? On the way back home I stopped off to check on 'Billy'.

'Oh,' said the farmer, 'he's fine, lad. He was sent off to Haggaback Farm to do a bit of mating. He didn't fancy it, so he tried to make his way back home.'

I don't blame him!

*

58

I was grateful for the shower block near my classroom and my PE track suit, which was always hanging up in my stock cupboard. I used them on a number of occasions. The first time was when, following a heavy snow fall, I attempted to make the journey from the moors to Hartlepool.

Thanks to snow blowers and snow ploughs, I managed to reach the main A171 Whitby to Guisborough road but the incline to Birk Brow was blocked. Not to be denied, I checked out a minor road on my right leading to Lingdale, Skelton and the coast.

About a hundred metres up this road, the local postman was standing near his little red van, his path blocked by the snow. 'If I can get through this bit, it will be easier down towards the coast,' he said.

Who was I to argue with local knowledge?

I always carried a shovel and wellies in the boot of my car, so with his shovel (of course he had one; he was a village postman delivering mail on the North York Moors) and mine, we set to.

The snow had stopped falling, the sun had come out, the sky had turned blue and it was glorious. I was really enjoying the experience and between us, following thirty minutes or so of furious shovelling, we opened a way through the twenty metres of blocked snow. We were now both dripping with sweat; he was down to his vest and I was minus my jacket, jumper, tie and shirt. Bare-chested with my shovel, I looked like a Newcastle United supporter in the Gallowgate end who had come to the match straight from the pit.

Did I get to school? Of course I did, much to the annoyance of staff who lived in Hartlepool and were stuck in their drives due to the snow and arrived later than me.

I was always early and gave myself time. It's easier to be late when you live next door – you can never make up the time.

*

In terms of living next door, I did indeed live next door to the village school at Castleton in a house called Glenfield, 40 High Street. How I longed for a job at the village school in spite of being so happy at Hartlepool.

I did have an interview for the headship of a village school (I think it was Kirby and Broughton) and I was one of two people called for the final interview. It was perhaps the cosiest interview I've ever had. It was held in the lounge of a house belonging to one of the governors. I was seated in an easy chair with the house cat brushing against my legs. Two of the interviewing panel were sitting on kitchen stools that had been brought in for the occasion, and another of the governors was sitting cross-legged on the floor. It was rather surreal but very relaxing.

It was a C of E school and I was not appointed. The person who was, was a church organist. I rest my case.

My disappointment was tempered by the tale of a friend of mine, John, who went for an interview for another village-school headship. He was successful but afterwards one of the governors, a rotund, red-faced man who happened to be the local butcher, said to him, 'Well done, son, but let me give you three pieces of advice. One: always have a good deputy. Two: never put anything personal down in writing. Three: never break wind in public!'

I suspect, as did my friend John, that this was his humorous, stock-in-trade welcome to all head-teacher appointees.

Welcome to the club, John!

6 School's Out

'...And, of course, remember you pass on the right!'

The owner of the canal-boat hire company.

If I had a penny for all the times holidays are mentioned after I say I was a teacher, I would be able to afford to go on holiday permanently. So as not to disappoint you, dear reader, here are a few tales of holidays and proof that terrifying tales did not end after I left the school premises.

In the days when Butlin's holiday camps were popular and dotted around our coasts, I spent one or two weeks there with Mum, Dad and my younger brother, Don. What struck me, when we visited the dining halls for our meals two or three times a day were those people waiting table. Those young men and women were neatly dressed, polite and seemed, come the end of the week, to do ever so well in terms of thank-yous and tips.

A few years later, during my student teacher days when the summer break arrived, I remembered those Butlin's days. Working at a holiday camp as a waiter would suit me down to the ground. I could do that. Plenty of smiles, chat to the children and parents, end of the week...

'Hope you have enjoyed your holiday and safe journey home. Oh, is that for me? Really, I couldn't. Well okay, thank you. That's very generous, you are most kind.'

What could be better? A chance to make a bit of money during the long holiday. Alas, it was not to be.

All was going smoothly as I entered the camp at Butlin's Filey in North Yorkshire, checked in at reception and was sent to get my gear. I stood in eager anticipation, waiting for my smart jacket, white shirt and trendy hat. Imagine my surprise when the first thing plonked on the counter at the staff-supplies office was a pair of rubber boots. They were followed by a navy boiler suit then a pair of thick rubber gauntlets.

'Kitchen's that way,' the man said. 'Just ask for the manager.'

What? There must be some mistake. I'm here to wait tables.

No, that was it: I was assigned to work in the kitchens and my primary task seemed to be that of scraping the thick grease off dozens of trays before washing them down in giant-sized sinks. This was unfair; I had been practising my friendly things to say for weeks. How could they do this to me?

Well, they did and it was quite an experience!

The characters I worked with were amazing. One was Rocky, a lad in his mid-twenties. He was very quiet but as solid as a boulder of granite from his native land of Scotland. When he spoke I could hardly understand him, so strong was his Scottish accent.

He was the most rectangular person I have ever encountered in terms of his shape. Starting from his shoulders, right down to the floor, he just seemed well … rectangular. When he wore his thick rubber apron, which almost touched the floor (he was not a tall man), this was even more pronounced. Even when he was dressed normally, he still had a kind of rectangular appearance.

Occasionally he would disappear into the huge walk-in freezers and come out chewing secretively on a chicken leg with a few bumps under his apron. I would guess that the bumps were more supplies for after work. Copying his actions crossed my mind but some of my work colleagues would quite easily have locked the door on me, so I didn't think it worth the risk. Rocky did not fear that happening because everyone was scared of him; also, I'm sure he would have bulldozed the door down with his head.

Then there was 'Miffy' (don't ask – I never did, so I couldn't tell you). Having spent most of the last five years in prison, so I was told, he had a habit of walking up behind you and dropping a whole pile of metal trays on the floor to the cry of 'Whoa!' Whenever he walked behind me with a pile of trays I closed my eyes and gritted my teeth in anticipation.

There were others, some with nicknames I could not repeat, certainly not for my well-respected readers.

I know the holiday camp strapline was: 'When it's raining it's fine at Butlin's!' I would tag on the line: 'But don't take shelter in the kitchens!'.

*

Before I was acquainted with these guys, something happened to me that was far more dramatic than anything they could have conjured up. In fact, it happened within thirty minutes of me donning my work apparel and setting off for my tasks.

Wearing my designer kitchen outfit, looking a picture in rubber, denim and cotton (the most ill-fitting set of clothing since Quasimodo said to Liberace, 'I'll just try on your jacket, I'm sure it's my size'), I strode over to the large sinks ready for action. On the floor in front of all the sinks were wooden slatted duck boards to stop us slipping on the greasy surface. They had the reverse effect; on placing my foot on them, I whizzed along the boards and aquaplaned into the side of a giant hot plate. This was NOT a sink but a hot plate ... a red-hot hot plate.

I was wearing my rubber gauntlets but my sleeves were rolled up to my elbows and my bare right arm flailed about as I sought to retain my balance. Smashing into the side of the hot plate, my arm came down on top of the searing hot area. The pain was so intense that I pushed my arm to my chest and ran to the kitchen exit. On reflection, I should have said, 'Excuse me, chaps, I'm frightfully sorry but I appear to have burned my arm on that beastly hot plate. Perhaps one of you could cut along to the first-aid centre and bring back a spot of cream and a bandage.'

Not really. I needed medical attention quickly. Fortunately, I remembered that the first-aid centre was close to the staff-supplies building so I ran in that direction as fast as I could. Sadly, the route was crowded. As I ran, I bumped into holidaymakers eating ice creams, candy floss and generally in good spirits. Maybe they were off to the Glamourous Granny competition or the Knobbly Knees event. I hadn't time to apologise as I barged my way through them. I couldn't have cared less – I was hurting badly.

I'm sure some of the holidaymakers thought it was a fun event, that one of the Redcoats had dressed up and was being chased by the camp kids. One or two were cheering and shouting as I charged through the crowd with my rubber boots flopping on the ground and my boiler suit flapping in the breeze.

'Yeah! Run, son – they're coming to get ye.'

'Go on, lad, you're in the lead.'

Big deal. They might have thought it funny but I didn't. Eventually I reached the medical centre and they were marvellous. Injections, medication, treatment on my badly burnt arm and the whole arm dressed in a sterile gauze that stayed on for a week or two.

After an hour or so, I returned to the kitchen and spoke with the boss. He had the impression I had just not fancied the work and had run away, as had the rest of the lads. I was given three or four days to recover and returned to my life of 'grime' later in the week. What an entrance!

It had compensations. The following day I was sitting in the Regency ballroom feeling sorry for myself when I noticed the fastening at the wrist of my dressing had worked loose. I also noticed that a pretty girl was sitting in front of me.

Should I? Why not? 'Excuse me, you couldn't fasten my bandage for me, could you?' Not the most awesome chat-up line.

She could and she did and we became good friends for a few weeks. It turned out she was a dancer in the variety shows and worked a punishing schedule. It was not at all the glamorous life style you might imagine – but neither was mine.

It wasn't the case of a romantic holiday fling, the grease-tray scraper and the show girl, but we met up from time to time for a coffee, mainly in mid-afternoon. After her showbiz stuff she was exhausted and went to bed asap. As for me, after 7pm I was also exhausted because, in addition to the kitchen work, I spent a lot of time on college assignments that had to be written up and worked on. Yes, I was conscientious. Don't believe all you have read about the swinging sixties; ninety per cent of it was a myth!

*

Then there was the 'holiday of holidays' several years later. I was married to my first wife and living in the lovely village of Castleton, North Yorkshire.

We had a decision to make. Let's have a holiday on a canal barge; let's go with our friends Bill and Anne; let's stay at home and paint the shed! On reflection, the third option would have been the wisest choice.

Bill, a lovely lad, owned a garage. He was a most gifted mechanic and was full of fun and high spirits. Always with a sense of adventure and into something different, it came as no surprise when he rolled up in a pink Jaguar motor car to take his wife, my wife and yours truly on our 'seafaring' – okay, canal – holiday. Actually, as it transpired it was more like an OK Corral holiday.

He reversed up the drive towards our home next to the village school and we started stowing our gear. It took an age but when we finished we were off Now, when I say we were off I mean we travelled all of two metres before we came to a shuddering halt. Well, you can't really move when one of your wheels has broken a manhole cover and has dipped six inches. Convert it into centimetres if you must, but I'll settle for six inches.

We were well and truly stuck!

After another movement of bodies and luggage, we had a lighter load. Bill, looking every inch like Parker, Lady Penelope's chauffeur from *Thunderbirds*, gently eased the car from the obstacle and the stowing began once more.

As we shared a drive, the neighbours were appeased and the situation explained, the broken manhole cover was moved to one side and off we went again. Reaching the boat yard, rather later than anticipated, we were shown to our floating home and given instructions on the finer points of canal barging. Personally, I would have preferred more guidance; considering what was to happen, I should have taken a week's tuition.

Chugging away, the monster barge moved away from the mooring post, pointy end first, blunt end at the rear. Nothing to it, I thought.

Slowly and steadily we travelled along, the ladies down below unpacking while Bill and I, the virgin bargees, got to grips with handling the vessel. Half an hour into the voyage and everything was going smoothly. The broken manhole cover incident was behind us and we were sailing to new horizons.

We had yet to pass, or be passed by, any other craft when Bill handed over the tiller to me, keen to see how I would handle the old tub. I certainly looked the part in my cable-stitch jumper and boating pumps. The icing on the cake was my white cotton cap with a black plastic peak above which sat a golden anchor.

'Ahoy there me hearties. Splice the main-brace, Jolly Roger, Captain Birdseye and all that stuff.' I was in my element. Until…

We were right in the middle of the canal and moving at a goodly rate of knots as we approached a curve to the right at a very wide bend in the river. Suddenly there in front coming towards us was a small pleasure cruiser, all white and chrome and glass. Strangely he was veering to my left. What on earth was he doing?

'Get over, man! Where are you going?'

He was going to my left. I was going to his right. Collision course.

I saw the *Titanic* and ice.

I saw the sinking of the *Belgrano*.

I saw disaster!

No, please don't let this happen.

But it did, as our powerful, weighty barge ploughed into the side of the little white cruiser not unlike a torpedo.

Smashing into his side, we (there's nothing like collective responsibility) rammed into him, pushing him into the riverbank and leaving a huge gaping hole amidships. I don't know if that's the correct term; at the time I couldn't have cared less. I had, to all intents and purposes, sunk a boat – in peace time!

Was it 'river rage'? Whatever it was, it was quite ugly. The pilot of the damaged vessel was inconsolable, shocked and, along with his wife, totally distraught. And a wee bit ANGRY.

Upset was not the word. I felt dreadful, especially when Bill told me that the rules of the road do not apply on a canal. I should have kept to the right as the damaged cruiser was doing.

Phone calls were made, the boat-hire pick-up van arrived on the towpath road and somehow, without going into finer details, things were resolved. The cruiser was a write off but we were okay and eventually we were on our way again.

I felt so sorry for the man and his wife whose holiday we had ruined. No one was injured but both parties were shaken. I was reluctant to go anywhere near the steering for a day or two. What a start to the holiday.

*

In addition to Bill's love of tinkering with motors were flying aeroplanes and driving rally cars, plus a spot of fishing. Not, as you might imagine, hauling in marlin off the deck of an ocean-going yacht; no, it was something much more down to earth with a small rod and line off our hired barge.

I assumed it was a relaxing pursuit and, after our adventures on the first day, I assumed it was much needed.

I was not, and I don't suppose I ever could be, an angler. Sitting for hours on end without a 'bite' would be so frustrating. No, I would need to be an angler like those in the television programmes where they are pulling in these flapping, flipping creatures every few minutes.

A day or two into our holiday and Bill was fishing contentedly, content in the fact that all was peace and quiet rather than in his success rate of catching fish. I cannot recall a single tiddler being landed. Indeed, if we had been relying on Bill to provide us with our dinner we would have perished due to malnutrition.

The bait he was using consisted of thousands of wriggly maggots, live bait as it were, squirming about in a cardboard shoe box. He was happy, the maggots (as far as I could tell) were happy, the rest of the crew were happy until…

It was early morning following a balmy sunny evening, with Bill fishing off the starboard side. (I'm not sure which side it was really but starboard side seems a sufficient nautical term to use.)

We woke from our slumbers to movement. Not to the movement of the barge; there was little movement when moored, save for the passing of other river craft. This was a different kind of movement – the movement everywhere of maggots!

Bill, it seems, had left the box of creepy crawlies on the top of the cabin overnight. A heavy rain shower, a cardboard shoe box not designed to resist a downpour and yippee, freedom.

The maggots were off the leash, so to speak. Like tenement-apartment dwellers on holiday, they threw off the shackles of being shoulder to shoulder with their maggoty mates and went rogue. They were everywhere, and I mean everywhere. There were so many of them that I'm sure they had invited their friends to join the fun.

A writhing mass of maggots… What is the collective term? A jelly of maggots? A wiggle of maggots?

Under cushions, under bedclothes, in cupboards, in clothes, on the ceiling, on the floor. Nothing was off limit to these guys, they were having a ball. Every surface was their playground and they were having fun. One of the girls held up her underwear to reveal further maggots.

Well, why not? If I was a maggot on the loose I cannot think of a finer place to snuggle into than a pair of ladies silk panties. But there again, having never been a maggot…

Hours later, having hosed down the decks and de-maggotted the interior, we were still discovering these tiny creatures eking out the last vestiges of freedom.

It was the termination of Bill's fishing, certainly for the canal trip!

At least I passed on the blame for this incident, but later in the afternoon…

My intentions were honourable. With the shiny, polished bargepole in hand, I was just about to place it back down on the deck at the side of the cabin, thinking it was safe to do so, when we seemed to increase speed. I didn't have time to move the pole to where it was stowed before a stone footbridge loomed up in front across the river.

Somehow the bargepole got stuck between the bulkhead (the sticky-up cabin thing on deck is the term for non-bargees, I think) and the fast-approaching apex of the bridge. There was a kind of creaking groan; as the bridge was solid and of a similar nature to the steel cabin structure, it was no contest.

The pole bent slowly; it was very quickly transformed from a straight bargepole into a rainbow shape. Suddenly there was a crack and a large portion of the pole rocketed into the air like a javelin, flying yards into the sky and landing like a spear, quivering in the middle of the farmer's field nearby.

At least the bridge was in one piece and the cabin hadn't moved. Sadly, we were 'up the creek without a bargepole'. This had to be rectified, as the bargepole was essential because of our steering skills, or lack of. Later that afternoon we passed a derelict old barge further upstream and spied a rather dirty pole lying on board this sad-looking craft, desperate for a home. Gladly we welcomed it aboard and, although not in the polished state of our former bargepole, the one that had just broken the Olympic javelin record, it served its purpose well.

After several duckings in the water and repeated handling in order to smooth the surface, the pole was as good as the one we had started with ... well almost!

*

Before I close the canal-holiday escapade with another 'classic' event, let me say that I am a wildlife lover. The last thing I would ever want to do is deprive butterflies of their food supplies – but sometimes needs must.

Our need on one of the mornings at the end of the eventful week was to find the keys to the barge, which had gone missing. I do not know who took responsibility for the keys disappearing but three versus one were the odds of me 'carrying the can'. I really don't know to this day who had the keys last but the point is that they were gone and without them we could not get into the cabin and could not start the engine.

The absent keys were only deemed missing as we made our way back to the barge from the canal-side pub where we had enjoyed our lunch. The pub was only about a hundred yards from the boat so we thought that retracing our steps might result in the missing keys turning up. Wrong: they didn't, in spite of searching high and low in the pub and along the towpath.

We then steadily made our way back to the barge in police fingertip-search mode.

I'm sure a quick phone call would have summoned someone from the hire company to bring a set of spare keys but, in view of our tragic start to the week, no one was prepared to make the call. We feared we had caused enough commotion. No, the keys would have to be found.

The towpath ran from our mooring to the place where we had lunched, a narrow stretch of tarmac with a slight slope down to the river. It was about two metres in all, consisting of a tangle of blackberry bushes and a lot of nettles. As the keys weren't in pockets, handbags, on the path or in the pub, we figured that they might have fancied playing hide and seek in the overgrown under-growth. We were desperate to find them.

To cut a long story – almost two hours, that's how long – short, we hacked and cut our way through this great swathe of greenery, suffering nettle stings, risking falling in the canal and generally entertaining passing river traffic and walkers. We had to use a variety of tools: bits of stick we found nearby; an odd length of pipe, and an old bike frame that was semi-submerged in the water.

Yes, we did find the keys under a dense patch of nettles about halfway from the barge to the pub just off the path. All I can say is that, in days to come, some council workmen gang whose task was to tidy up the river-bank foliage would have had time to drink an extra cup of tea and claim on their time sheet for work that we had done. No problem, guys, have it on us!

I have never ever stepped on board a sea-going, or indeed canal-going vessel, again. Well, are you surprised?

7 Heads I Win

*'Could I just have a look at your
coal bunker in the yard?'*

(To fellow Head during an appraisal meeting)

Since having my first book published, it has been an absolute joy meeting up with so many people linked with school over the past fifty years. These encounters have stirred the memory of tales that happened so long ago.

'Do you remember when…?'

'How about when…?'

For those people who jogged my memory, here are some missing headship tales from my first book, equally true and equally horrific. And for those of you who reminded me of events that I have not put in print, surely they were the ones that no one would possibly think happened – even to me.

I suppose my strength was that I liked to be out of my office and in the school at the chalk face, as it used to be called. (Yes, it does rather date me, doesn't it?)

Out of my office one day, with sleeves rolled up, I was taking some empty cardboard boxes to the bin compound just off the staff car park. This task was usually dealt with by Rob, the school caretaker, but he was sorting out a burnt-out motor bike in the yard. It was a Monday morning, the secretary was dealing with the usual flurry of parent activity and I was not content to have the litter of boxes in the reception area.

After a number of trips with the cardboard boxes, I noticed a delivery wagon reversing through the gates and into the centre of the rows of parked cars. There were thirty or forty cars and I decided to guide him to a safe spot.

'Hey, mate, give us a hand with this stuff.'

'That's fine,' I replied. 'I think they're the chairs we've been waiting for.'

'Just put them over there. I'll take this to the office,' the driver said, waving some papers at me.

'I'll sign the delivery note,' I said.

'No, if you just put them over there, I need to go to the loo. The Head can sign it if he's not sitting on his a*** reading the paper!'

'Oh, he won't be doing that, he's busy helping the delivery man.'

'Hey, I'm sorry, pal. I thought you were the caretaker.' he muttered in an embarrassed way.

'No trouble,' I laughed. 'You go to the loo.'

I didn't mind and I bet he repeated this story many times in the weeks to come. I would have done so if I'd been him.

*

The delivery man's mistake was no big deal and only affected two people, him and me. The mistake that I made, along with my two Y6 members of staff, was one that affected the two teachers and their respective classes.

It stemmed from the fact that we had assumed that a well-known children's author would be ideally suited to speak to children about his books and stories. Not so; in fact, one hundred per cent not so!

Came the day of his visit, and we chatted in my office before I took him along to meet the members of staff and the fifty or sixty children he would talk to. They had assembled in one of the classrooms, where I left them for the next hour or so. I wished I could have stayed and heard him speak and not had to attend yet another meeting in my room.

When my meeting ended, I dashed along to the classroom. As soon as I opened the classroom door, I knew that things weren't as they should be. In fact, I was presented with a room full of pupils who were unsettled and fidgeting. I'm not surprised: he had bored the pants off them. He was great at writing children's stories but at connecting verbally with children he was a non-starter.

As I sat down next to one of the members of staff, this was made quite evident as she waved four fingers across her throat and whispered to me, 'Get rid of him!'

Pretty conclusive, I thought.

Within five minutes, I had made an excuse of one class having to go swimming or having to attend a cookery demonstration or preparing for a trip to Outer Mongolia – anything to rescue the situation.

The damage had been done, however, and I was relieved when the author left the assembled group and walked back to my room with me. I was relieved – and the staff and children certainly were.

It was a lesson to be learned for the future. Adults may well sit in awe of their heroes, sporting or otherwise, and politely accept any offering from the person they have put on a pedestal. Children are far more discerning and not fooled as easily.

Here was the proof big time!

*

Another error of judgement came when I thought the parents in the school, of which I was head, would have the same sense of humour as me.

Let me explain. A new initiative from above called the National Curriculum was to be phased in. In order to outline what this would mean, schools hosted a series of meetings to explain to parents the implication of this government-initiated strategy and what it would mean to their children.

Fellow heads had varying success in attracting parents to meetings. How could we attract our parents? My idea was to put on invitation cards the title *An Evening with Natt Curric* and add to this text an illustration of a champagne glass with bouncy little bubbles.

Certainly the invitation aroused interest though, to be fair, most of the parents had done their homework, so to speak, and had an idea it was a trap. All except one or two, who came dressed as though it were a cocktail party.

The hall wasn't exactly full but maybe there were more parents than we would have had if not for the title of the invitation. I gave an outline of the National Curriculum, how it would be phased in and when. Question and answers followed … then we drank champagne and nibbled our canapes. Not really; obviously we had tea and biscuits.

My biggest problem on that evening was discovering that my reading glasses had gone AWOL about five minutes before I delivered my talk. Panic ensued and, after a frantic search, the glasses were found just before the meeting commenced.

The 'Evening with Nat Curric' and similar introductions were just the start for all schools and the 'show' goes on to this day, ever popular with teachers and educators throughout the land.

Just ask them … if you dare!

*

The National Curriculum was just one of a number of new things thrown at schools. A rigorous appraisal system was introduced for staff, with head teachers appraising their fellow heads.

Who would I be scrutinising and be scrutinised by? Well, would you believe it, the head teacher of Thornaby Village school, where it had all started for me in the infants' school years earlier – more than forty years earlier!

Let me say from the onset that TW (the head) was a lovely lad and a lot younger than me, I hasten to add. His was a high-tech office with wall-to-wall computers, flashing lights and gadgets of all kinds. Mine had football boots in the corner, a silver cup on one of the shelves and a bookcase … traditional.

My first question was certainly an icebreaker: 'Hi, before we start, could I see your coal bunker?'

Moving to the yard there it stood, I was transported back to my infant days. Wow, was that it? The huge coal bunker was so high that I could step on it by lifting my foot a matter of centimetres. This had been my childhood challenge; we had no hopscotch bays or painted wiggly-worms or number squares or the hundred-and-one playground markings children now have to help them in their play. How I would have loved those things.

The good old days! Well, I'm not so sure. The rosy hues of nostalgia can quickly fade when the reality of what really was kicks in.

Mind you, I did love leaping off that coal bunker. It was such fun.

*

One of the pleasant things I found was speaking to children in assemblies and telling a wide variety of stories. Children do love being told stories and, if the story is well read or told from memory in an interesting way, they will listen and listen well and enjoy. Indeed, it is something that children find pleasurable, sharing a story being told to them in a group.

It is not all about electronic screens, flashing lights and weird noises ... or am I being old-fashioned?

So, there I was telling a Christmas story in the hall to two hundred plus children, the Upper Year 3 to 6, on a fairly gloomy pre-Christmas morning in December. Not a sound but my voice; not a murmur from the children. Staff were seated around the hall; the walls and displays were looking beautifully Christmassy. The children were anticipating the last few days of parties, concerts, film shows etc., etc., the usual trappings that were part and parcel of our wind down to Christmas and the holiday.

The Advent candles on the assembly table cast a warm glow on the faces of the younger children seated cross-legged on the front row. It was a veritable picture of Christmas peace.

What could go wrong?

Well, the Advent candles could set fire to the imitation greenery on the table, the tablecloth with robins and holly embroidered on them could add more flames to the proceedings, and the certificates, my notices and spectacle case could also join in the fun.

That's what could go wrong.

It happened so quickly: the faint burning smell; the

gasp from the children. I was always good at telling stories, and the response from the children proved this on many occasions, but why were they not fixing their gaze on me?

Because the assembly table was going up in smoke!

Before a child could move, before members of staff left their chairs, I leapt across the floor and gathered the four corners of the tablecloth and the contents of the table into a bundle and raced for the boys' loo. Fortunately, the boys' toilets were just outside the large hall and an ideal place for the bundle of Advent flames.

It was a dramatic conclusion to the assembly but no one was injured – though my shirt was a wee bit blackened at the cuffs.

Holy smoke. I swear that phrase never entered my head!

The village church I now attend has large candles on the altar and, rest assured, I am always ready to act as a surrogate fireman whenever they are lit!

*

For many years, before stepping back once more into schools as an adult, I worked with children and young people in a Sunday School at Billingham Methodist Church. Around this time, I ran the 'Inters' youth club at the church for children aged between ten and fourteen years of age and thoroughly enjoyed being with these youngsters. This led to me being appointed a youth leader at Billingham Community Centre.

During this time, following a training and study programme linked to my centre work, I gained my youth leader's certificate. It was great fun. I coached football teams, ran a drama group (which, incidentally, came runner-up in a local festival after an outstanding performance) and, having acquired a guitar, developed a folk singing group.

Mentioning guitar playing... My guitar playing was limited, to say the least. In fact, there is a little story that allows me to name drop and to emphasise how a certain young man, Edwin Jobson, ruined my guitar-playing development.

Eddie (whose dad was a head teacher, I believe) was a member of my Inters Club. I got on so well with this little guy, and clearly he was impressed with my guitar-playing skills! Yes, all three of the chords that I could just about manage.

He would sit in the coffee-bar area, listening to me playing.

Me thinking: 'He thinks I'm great on guitar.'

Eddie thinking: 'He is rubbish. I could do better.'

The second thought was proved when I bought a new guitar and gave Eddie my old one.

Within three weeks (three weeks!) he was playing it far better than me and he was only thirteen or fourteen years of age. I comfort myself with the thought that it is not so much a reflection on my lack of ability so much as Eddie's phenomenal musicality.

Gradually my guitar playing faded and I turned my attention to pursuits in which I would gain far greater success – basket weaving, jigsaw puzzling and train spotting, to name but a few.

Eddie, you may be pleased to know, went on to become a world-famous, progressive-rock musician featuring on keyboards, violin and synthesizer. He played for bands such as Curved Air, Roxy Music, Jethro Tull and was part of Frank Zappa's band, which was outstanding in the

1970s.

All this was brought to mind as he was on the 6pm north-east news programme recently, having been inducted into the American Rock Hall of Fame. In fact, the programme came on television right in the middle of writing this chapter. Eddie always had a great sense of timing and he's done it again. Cheers, 'Jobbo'.

I wonder if he's read my book. Maybe he'll mention it to his rock-star friends… 'Hey, man, just read a cool book by a cat called Bryan. Used to know him years ago. You must read it, dude, it'll clear freak you out!' (That's how these music stars speak … isn't it.)

I believe he is still strutting his stuff and has a music studio in America. I'm sure I've heard my musical influence in some of his music. Eddie, you owe me, son.

By the way, Eddie, if you're reading this, did you know I am a fully paid-up member of the Eskuleles, a ukulele band from the Castleton and Danby area in North Yorkshire? Oh yes, Mr Jobson, you're not the only one who has made it big!

Roxy Music? Never heard of 'em.

*

You may well be wondering why I have included this tale of Eddie in this section. He was part of my initial work with youngsters and, had the club experience not happened, I wouldn't have even considered going into teaching.

In my first book there is a reference to an incident that happened in a youth club that I will explain later. This was linked to an event that happened when I was leading Tilery Youth Club on premises in the grounds of Tilery Primary School, as it is now. They were then separate infant and junior schools.

By then I was actually in a teaching post at my first school and had been invited to develop a youth club on the Portrack estate. I was head-hunted before I even became a Head!

Basically, the building was a twin classroom block situated on an area of grassland between the infant and junior schools. One half of the building was a kind of games room, with a table-tennis and pool tables and a dartboard. The other room was a coffee-bar area with small tables and chairs for more relaxing activities.

The age range was supposedly from ten to fourteen but in actual fact children of all primary and secondary school ages – and even some toddlers – came along. We had one young man, Mike Finch, who played in goal for one of the two football teams we ran (11–14 and 16–18) who made three or four appearances for Hartlepool United Football Club in the football league.

The place was packed to overflowing and the activities and events we were involved in were truly incredible.

Sadly, the youth club had had a less than auspicious start. I'm not surprised. The place had opened a few months before I was appointed and whoever was running it had pinned up a sheet of paper in the entrance hall saying things like:

- No running inside the building.
- No throwing chairs.
- No spitting.
- No swearing.
- No fighting.

The youngsters who came along thought these instructions were the opposite of good ideas and decided to give them all a go. No wonder the place came to a halt after a few weeks.

The first thing I did was to rip up these rules. It didn't exactly solve all the problems but, with two assistant leaders, Marge and later Judith, who were great with the youngsters, we turned things round and the atmosphere and enjoyment in and around the place were wonderful.

I can recall quite clearly driving away from the first session with about half a dozen youngsters hanging onto the back of my little green Mini and thinking 'I'm not coming back here again'… but I did.

I'm pleased that I did, for we enjoyed some wonderful years. When I left, due to teaching promotions, it was so very hard to say goodbye. The youngsters there had become good friends and quite a few tears were shed (more by me than anyone else) on my final evening when the members gave me many lovely farewell gifts.

But back to the incident I referred to a few paragraphs ago.

It was a mid-summer evening. We were coming to the end of an evening youth club session and I was playing a game of rounders with boys and girls on the grass outside the building. The ball was hit towards the infant school building and one of the boys went to field it.

As the boy picked up the tennis ball from under the window of the school, he noticed water on the floor of the school building. I left them playing their game and investigated. Looking in through other windows, I discovered that water was indeed covering some of the classroom floors.

Should I break in and investigate further? No, perhaps

not. Earlier in this book you will recall I tried that in my first appointed school and was caught.

I hadn't a clue where the caretaker lived but, as Marge was locking up and the children were on their way home, they were all keen to tell me, 'She'll be in the pub'.

On their advice I went to the local pub and, sure enough, she was there in front of her beverage. To cut a long story short, she went back home and gathered her bunch of keys.

We entered the school building. Certainly there was a leak and water was dripping from the ceiling of one of the classrooms.

I persuaded the caretaker to get some ladders, though in all honesty I can't recall from where we collected them. Having done so, I placed them up against the ceiling trapdoor in one of the rooms of this old high-ceilinged, classroom building. I said I would check it out. The caretaker seemed keen to return to the pub, maybe to pay the tab and finish her drink. I didn't know but I assumed that, once she'd done what she was going to do, she would return within a few minutes.

Up in the loft area above the classrooms was more of a challenge than I'd envisaged. There were dust and cobwebs everywhere and I had to be careful not to miss my footing and fall through the ceiling. Luckily I was quite fit and my balance was sure.

Though it was quite gloomy in the loft space, I located the leak. Now, I am not a plumber but I could see a length of piping that seemed to be leaking at the point where two pieces were joined. I cleaned the joint, applied some flux, gently heated the matching ends and taped the seal securely (joking!). What I actually did was shove the two pieces together as firmly as I could. It stopped the dripping water so I was pleased. Sorted!

Feeling akin to the boy who put his finger in the dyke, I descended the ladders keen to inform the caretaker that I had done my bit. On reflection, I should have had someone holding the ladders for me but, being quite athletic and steady on my feet, I skipped down them like a two year old, as they say.

Three rungs from the bottom, however, I slipped. Perhaps the smooth-soled trainers didn't help! There I was, lying on my back in an inch or two of water, the light fading rapidly and with no lights switched on for fear of electrical problems. All the youngsters had gone and the youth club was locked up. I was alone.

'What if the leak starts again and I drown?' I asked myself. 'What if the caretaker decides to have another drink and forgets about me?'

I lay there, wet, dazed and wondering if I had been damaged in any way. On reflection, it must have only been for a minute or two. Then I gave myself a stern talking-to. 'Come on, you do not have any pain. You are just wet, a bit shaken and feeling stupid.' Eventually I eased myself to my feet, squelched my way to the door and met the caretaker walking along the school drive.

'All sorted for the time being,' I said, explained things to her in a bit more detail and left.

I learned later that she did a bit of mopping up and the maintenance men arrived early the next morning, which fortunately was a Saturday, to see to things properly.

I drove home with the back of my clothing wet and some of the front rather moist too.

The head teacher of the school, although I did not know it at the time, happened to be Mrs L, the teacher who was my next-door teaching colleague in my first year. What a small, small world.

She sent me a letter via one of the pupils at the junior school who also happened to be a youth club member. In typical head-teacher speak, it was very formal but it was a thank you which I appreciated. A phrase in the letter went along the lines of: *for taking prompt action and preventing further damage to the fabric of the school…*

Thanks, June. I never told her that it was me, the rookie teacher from years gone by!

Another quirk of fate happened a few months ago when June turned up at the launch of my first book at Fens Primary school in Hartlepool. It was such a joy to see her.

I bought her some flowers … and gave her a hug.

8 Memories and Reflections

I was prompted to write this final chapter in my final book of teaching memoirs to remember past friends in schools that I worked in and who are sadly no longer with us. Appropriately, I am writing this two days before the hundred-year Remembrance Day tributes of November 2018.

Over the past weeks I have seen on television and witnessed in person some wonderfully creative poppy displays in my home town of Stockton-on-Tees and my present home, Castleton. In shops, schools, churches of all denominations, pubs and on memorial crosses the displays have been such a tribute to the men and women who gave their lives. Such poignant reminders.

As I write, how sad it is that over this memorial period I have read of acts of vandalism in a local special-needs school, a man of ninety-eight years of age being attacked and robbed in his own home, stabbings in London and acts of terrorism. In the main, these atrocities have been committed by citizens of this land, people related to families for whom these brave soldiers gave their lives. It is a truly sobering thought.

Do we blame the schools? Television as part of the general media influence? Society at large? Politicians, and so on?

I don't know. I am not qualified, or indeed knowledgeable enough, to make any assumptions but I do consider how we can prepare our children to go into a world such as this to face the challenges that await them.

There are no easy answers but homes and schools are

two of the major platforms, with parents and teachers the two groups of key players.

*

2019 is upon us and I raise a glass to absent friends, friends who have passed on, without whom life in school over the years would have been so much more difficult, less satisfying and far less enriching.

Few people reading this book will know them but those who do will understand why I write these tributes because you will have been blessed and encouraged by them as I have been.

Mr (Ernie) Clark (Frederick Nattrass School) A wonderful man – generous, kind and thoughtful. I could not have had a better role model for a head teacher.

He was supportive in all that I did. My thanks to him for saving my skin on my first day with an unruly pupil. He used to interrupt my Monday morning teaching sessions so I could give him a match report of the school teams' performances on the previous Saturday if he had been unable to attend the game.

I am grateful that he was there one Saturday as we travelled home from the 'wilds' of County Durham, having been beaten 3–2 in the quarter-final of Durham County Primary Cup. (I think it was our tenth match in the competition). Our coach load of pupils, parents and I were all feeling down but his presence was a great help.

He was a master of the 'bread-and-butter' stuff and exceptional in the ways in which he handled staff and pupils: guiding, supporting, even challenging and chastising them (me included) where necessary.

Even when he had retired and his handwriting was scrawling, scratchy and difficult to read, he sent me such encouraging letters, especially when I was going through some bad times. I still have them.

Margaret Herbert (Fens School) A teacher at Fens School, Hartlepool, Margaret had many qualities but I remember her most for stopping me from giving up my teaching job.

I returned to school on the day before school started for the children following a holiday, all set to walk away from my deputy headship following a traumatic period in my life.

As I sat with my head on my desk and in such a state, Margaret came into my classroom. Even though she had such a lot of preparation to do, she spent almost two hours talking to me, encouraging and motivating me to carry on. What a blessing she was that day and in the years to come.

Elsie Mould A neighbour at Castleton who showed such love and care when I found myself having to live on my own. Never fussy, intrusive or uncaring, she was always there for me. She was another person who kept me going during a difficult school year.

Those who knew her don't need me to tell them what a good person she was. Over the past eighteen months since I moved back to Castleton, whenever I've mentioned her to anyone they have all said the same – what a lovely lady she was. Never a wrong word about her.

Sheila Simpson (Grange School) Sheila was a teacher at Grange Junior School where I started my first headship. Loyal and dedicated, she worked so hard with the children at the school.

She gave such a lot to the pupils and, in her own time and through her own efforts, guided our Road Safety Quiz team not only to win the Hartlepool Final but to win the Cleveland Primary Schools Final. It was a splendid effort by the children but also recognition of the work and application of a first-class teacher colleague.

Wyn Walton (Grange Infant School) Wyn was the head teacher of Grange Infants School when I was appointed head of the junior school and she was marvellous. She kept me right. She was a jolly, exuberant lady, full of fun – but not one to mess with. Wyn was also there to advise and guide me when the two schools were amalgamated under my leadership as a large primary school.

I was always glad to welcome her back to school. She never undermined my authority and she was a gem. We always had her back at Christmas time, thumping out her merry tunes on the piano for the parties. My lasting impression was of her huge frame perched on the piano stool, a glittery little bowler hat on her head, being adored by all the pupils.

Replace Wyn? I never could, nor would I want to.

Mr Robert Prichard- ROZ (Tilery School) Last but not least – in fact, this is where we came in, as they say.

Mr Prichard started round about the same time as I did more than fifty years ago at Freddy Natt school. I had completed my first year when this giant of a man came along – what a character! In truth, our school couldn't handle him, not even my hero Mr Clark.

Mr Prichard only lasted a year with us before he moved on to Tilery School and the legend began. He stayed there for the whole of his full-time career; he was most certainly a one-off!

Roz was the name by which he was known to staff, pupils, parents and friends alike. He was never Mr Prichard; in fact, most of them, especially the pupils, would have been hard put to recognise that name.

I don't know when it started, but his traditional dress was a long, flowing academic gown, which accentuated his six-feet-plus height, adorned by his bow tie. Oh, and of course his highly polished boots.

He was worshipped by pupils past and present and known as 'Mr Tilery'. Ask anyone who lives on Portrack housing estate about Roz, unless they moved in within the past week, and their eyes will light up and they will have a tale to tell.

I lost track of Roz, teaching-wise, but I lived quite nearby and often we would bump into each other on the street and chat for a long time. He was always a pleasure to meet and he showed interest in what I was doing, my family and especially my two boys.

The wheel turned full circle when I spent one or two years doing a few odd days' supply teaching at his school, Tilery. What fun it was to meet up again; we even starred as Munchkins in the school *Wizard of Oz* production. Of course, it was with such mixed feelings that I was there at his farewell assembly. Children entered the hall resplendent in bow ties, every single one of the 200-plus pupils.

Towards the end of his life it was a privilege to visit him in hospital, respite centre and in his own home.

Personally, it is fitting that I should start and end my teaching career in schools with Roz. I cannot think of a person with whom I would rather start and end my school journey and my book.

*

So, to finish. As with my first book I bring the final chapters to a poetic conclusion and end with a poem I wrote reflecting life's journeying. But before I venture into verse, may I add that if a third book is forthcoming it will, in all probability, be a book of my poems, *Quit While You're a Poet!* Of course, this will only be possible if my path of life continues and a few more words are written before the final full stop.

Many of my poems feature my local Teesside area; they have an element of humour although I have written one or two with my 'serious head' on.

More Milligan than Masefield, more Belloc than Betjeman and certainly more Lear than Longfellow. I'm sure you will enjoy reading them,

The Paths of Life

The 'paths of life' are moved along each day.
A solitary lane,
A dusty track,
A wide highway.

The 'paths of life', each day a different gait.
A toddler's tread-unsure, yet unafraid,
Or bound and leap of youth,
Who cannot wait.

The prime of life, the time of life,
When each step is a sure,
Purposeful stride,
A confidence with eyes full open wide.

The 'paths of life' each year at differing pace.
A pensioner's plod,
Cautious, a knowing shuffle,
No hurry – horizons near, destination clear?

No map could plot the route we'll take.
Each daily challenge,
A hard or easy section,
Will move us to some new direction!

The 'paths of life', a blessing or a curse?
A pleasant stroll,
A stumbling fall,
Sometimes when things are bad, they could be worse.

The 'paths of life' in sunshine or in rain.
An uphill struggle,
A downward trek,
A feeling that I'll never pass this way again.

The 'paths of life' have crossroads, junctions by the score.
We waver, make decisions,
Discard, accept – go right, go left,
Or move in ways, as done before.

The 'paths of life' each day will wend.
Arrow straight or sudden bend,
We'll walk the path but never know
Just when the path will end.

What travellers have you met along your paths of life?
Have they brought you joy and happiness, or sorrow, grief and strife?
Have you said hello and left them? Have they walked with you some way?
Destined to stay by your side, with you each passing day.

I'm curious looking back on life, more curious each

day.
How things would have looked if only I'd walked another way,
If I'd gone here, if I'd gone there, if I'd stopped and
thought a while.
If I'd run, slowed down or met up with that stranger –
if I'd gone another mile.

I can ponder, I can puzzle
With such cu-ri-osi-ty,
But if I'd not travelled as I did,
I'd simply not-be-me!

CONCLUSION

A friend of mine on hearing of my literary pursuits remarked, 'Bet you haven't mentioned ****** in your book,' and proceeded to challenge me to refer and insert this unmentionable word.

Well, Mr Smarty Pants, I will and in doing so win my bet… and exit with…

'BREXIT'!